Dear S.O.S.:
D E S S E R T
RECIPE
REQUESTS
TO THE LOS ANGELES TIMES

ROSE DOSTI

Los Angeles Times
A Times Mirror Company

Los Angeles, California

𝕷𝖔𝖘 𝕬𝖓𝖌𝖊𝖑𝖊𝖘 𝕿𝖎𝖒𝖊𝖘

Publisher: Richard T. Schlosberg III
Editor: Shelby Coffey III

Los Angeles Times Syndicate
President and CEO: Jesse Levine
VP/GM Domestic: Steve Christensen

Director of Book Development: Don Michel
Book Editor: Lauren Beale
Book Designer: Patricia Moritz

Library of Congress Catalogue Number: 96-77741
ISBN 1-883792-15-0
Copyright © 1996 Los Angeles Times

Published by Los Angeles Times Syndicate
Times Mirror Square, Los Angeles, California 90053
A Times Mirror Company

First printing September 1996

Printed in the U.S.A.

CONTENTS

ACKNOWLEDGMENTS

A huge debt of gratitude is due to all past and present editors, copy editors and the Los Angeles Times test kitchen staff who, for the last 30 years, have been testing, correcting and developing recipes. Special thanks go to The Times present kitchen staff, home economist and Times test kitchen director Donna Deane and assistant Mayi Brady, who tested numerous recipes and cleared up questions. The first Culinary SOS editor Anita Bennett and successor Cecil Fleming, who wrote the column until their retirements, as well as former staffers Minnie Bernadino, Judy Masters, Helen Stefanac and many assistants, all deserve thanks.

INTRODUCTION

Surprising as it may seem in this age of concern over fat intake, calories, sugar and salt, more Los Angeles Times readers of the Culinary SOS food column ask for dessert recipes than any other category of dishes.

Our national obsession with gooey, chewy, luscious offerings is reflected in this book. Readers ask for chocolate more than any other flavor and oatmeal cookies more than any other type. The recipes here are the most frequently requested, most popular desserts from the three-decade history of the column.

Every recipe in the book has withstood the test of time and they have been repeatedly tested in The Times test kitchen over a period of many years. Sometimes, changes have been made to accommodate modern health standards. For instance, unless critical to the recipe, we have virtually eliminated giving the exact amount of salt in favor of salting to taste when applicable. At one point, margarine was the preferred fat. Today butter is preferred, unless the recipe specifies otherwise. Old-time recipes made with lard have been almost completely eliminated.

The reason why these recipes have made the cut and others have not is simple: They work under the most universal conditions and accommodate the wide range of skills of our readers. For the most part, the recipes use the fewest number of ingredients possible and they are economical in terms of time and expense. That's not to say there are no complex and expensive recipes. However, the overall focus is simplicity and economy.

Where do the recipes come from? Many sources have contributed to this book. Many recipes were developed in The Times test kitchen when a source refused to share a recipe, as was the case for an orange drink so satisfying it doubles as dessert. Our own files going back to the '40s have produced such economical favorites as *Devil's Food Cake* and *Poor Man's Cake*. The famous Brown Derby restaurant was responsible for the ever-popular *Grapefruit Cake* recipe. Former First Lady Eleanor Roosevelt contributed her recipe for *Blueberry Pudding*. Actor Vincent Price so impressed a restaurant he dined at with praise of his own bread pudding that they tried it. The pudding remains a top-selling item at the restaurant to this day.

A reader contributed a country fair blue-ribbon prize recipe for pumpkin cake. The Pillsbury Bake-Off introduced *Tunnel of Fudge Cake*, which had to be reformulated when the cake mix was discontinued. A cake mix label also produced *Piña Colada-White Coconut Cake*. An airline was the source for a macadamia nut-carrot cake. An old Boston Cooking School magazine from the turn of the century gave us the basic formula for *Zwieback Toast*. *Chinese Fortune Cookies* came from a Chinese bakery in Los Angeles. No one ever expected a recipe from a hospital to become as popular as

Martin Luther King Hospital Oatmeal Cookies. And, frankly, we never anticipated hearing from Hillary Rodham Clinton when we requested a recipe for her *Chocolate Chip-Oatmeal Cookies*. She sent the recipe along with a photograph of her dog, who, we assumed, loved the cookies as much as our readers.

The book is filled with lost, then found, recipes. One day we put out an SOS of our own, asking readers if anyone had our recipe for soft sugar cookies called *World's Best Sugar Cookies*. Literally hundreds of readers came to our rescue with recipes, many of the copies yellowed with age.

One reader, whose dog chewed up her recipe for *Amaretto-Chocolate Cheesecake*, requested a reprint. Still another reminded us that *Vacuum Cleaner Cookies* were also called *Neiman Marcus Squares*, because the recipe cost $200 to purchase or so the story goes. (We never were able to verify the story, and the Neiman Marcus people say they never charged anyone for the recipe.)

Once, when a reader requested a recipe for *Hayden's Rice Pudding*, we identified it as one that had come from a restaurant. Several irate readers insisted that the recipe originated from the late actor Sterling Hayden. We decided to credit both in the hopes that one day we will discover the truth about Hayden's Rice Pudding.

Anecdotes are part and parcel of this book. They give life and breath to the recipes. Our goal is for each and every cook to have as much fun reading the recipes as they have cooking them at home.

A word of warning when preparing desserts: Be sure to follow cake recipes exactly or chemical changes could alter the texture and taste. Many baked products rely on strict ingredient formulation, and any tampering can spell trouble. Play it safe and stick to the recipe. You can, however, experiment with other desserts, such as fruit desserts, when flavors are a question of taste.

We have endeavored to avoid errors in reproducing these recipes. However, things can and do go wrong under the best of circumstances even when the recipe is foolproof and the cook is experienced. We have known famous chefs whose soufflés did not rise and whose cakes fell. Weather and room or oven temperatures can often affect baked products. Improper beating, folding or stirring can also have an adverse effect on a product. Over- and under-cooking are other factors that can make a difference.

To help prevent common pitfalls, we've included several useful guides and charts. Glance at the section *How to Use the Recipes* before starting the book. The section on *Preparation Techniques* describes methods used in dessert making that will help avoid problems. The *Table of Equivalents* is helpful if you need to double or triple a recipe. The *Purchasing Guide* can be used to help compare cup, ounce and pound measures. A brief *Glossary of Terms* will help clarify methods of preparation.

❖

CAKES

We receive more requests for cakes than any other type of dessert, which begs the question of the public's obsession with weight control and low-fat and low-calorie foods. Still, the requests keep coming, and we keep providing readers with their favorite cake recipes. We have been amazed at the longevity of certain recipes over the years. Moreover, nostalgic cakes, such as *Hot Fudge Pudding Cake* or *Fruit Cocktail Cake*, are easy enough for any novice to tackle.

There is a cake recipe for everyone, no matter what level of skill or what taste preferences. Some may enjoy the cakes made from commercial mixes, such as *Pina Colada-White Coconut Cake* or a delicious cake with the audacious name *Better Than Sex Cake*, whose origin is still a mystery. Veteran bakers will enjoy numerous roll-up-your sleeves recipes, including a version of *Lindy's New York Cheesecake* baked in a cookie crust.

Dear S.O.S.:
You once printed a recipe for a chocolate cake made with prunes. It sounds awful but I hear it's great. Do you still have the recipe?
—Mrs. S.T.

Dear Mrs. S.T.:
Loma Linda University food service people developed this unusual cake with terrific flavor and texture results. Who, indeed, would have thought?

CAKE MIX BASED

AMARETTO CUSTARD CAKE

The added appeal of this Amaretto-flavored cake is that it is made with cake mix and instant pudding mix.

> *1 (18 1/2-ounce) package yellow cake mix*
> *1 (3-ounce) package instant vanilla pudding mix*
> *2 eggs*
> *1 1/4 cups milk*
> *1/4 cup Amaretto or Amaretto and Cognac*
> *1/4 teaspoon ground nutmeg*
> *Glaze*

Combine cake mix, pudding mix, eggs, milk, Amaretto and nutmeg in large bowl and beat at low speed, scraping bowl constantly, 1 minute. Beat on medium speed, scraping bowl occasionally, 2 minutes.

Pour into greased and floured 12-cup Bundt cake pan. Bake at 350 degrees 40 to 45 minutes, until wood pick inserted in center comes out clean. Cool 15 minutes. Remove from pan. Drizzle with Glaze.

> **GLAZE**
>
> *1 1/2 cups powdered sugar*
> *2 tablespoons Amaretto or Amaretto and Cognac*
> *2 tablespoons milk or half and half*
> *Dash nutmeg*
> *Dash salt*

Mix sugar, Amaretto, milk, nutmeg and salt until glaze is smooth and of drizzling consistency.

BETTER THAN SEX CAKE

Despite the dubious title, the cake has been a great favorite for at least a decade. The cake and its many improvisations probably circulated in the Southeastern Seaboard and passed across the country through food editors.

1 (18.5 ounce) package yellow cake mix
1 (1-pound 4-ounce) can crushed pineapple
1 cup sugar
1 (6-ounce) package vanilla pudding mix
1 cup whipping cream, whipped and sweetened
Flake coconut, lightly toasted

Prepare cake in 13 x 9-inch baking pan and bake according to package directions. Combine crushed pineapple and sugar in saucepan and bring to boil. Cool slightly. When baked cake has cooled, poke holes in it with fork. Pour pineapple mixture over it. Prepare pudding mix according to package directions. Cool. Spread prepared pudding over top. Chill.

Just before serving, cover with sweetened whipped cream and sprinkle with coconut. If desired, garnish with pineapple slices. Makes 12 to 16 servings.

Notes:

EGGNOG CAKE

A great way to use leftover eggnog.

> *1 regular-size package yellow cake mix*
> *2 eggs*
> *1 ½ cups dairy eggnog*
> *¼ cup butter or margarine, melted*
> *½ teaspoon ground nutmeg*
> *½ teaspoon rum extract*
> *Eggnog Filling*
> *Whipped Cream Frosting*
> *Nutmeg, optional*
> *Red and green maraschino cherries, optional*

Use cake mix calling for 2 eggs and 1⅓ cups water. Combine cake mix, eggs, eggnog, butter, nutmeg and rum extract in large mixer bowl. Beat 4 minutes. Pour batter into 2 wax paper-lined greased and floured 8-or 9-inch cake pans. Bake at 375 degrees 30 minutes or until cake tester comes out clean. Cool 10 minutes, turn out onto wire rack and cool thoroughly.

Spread cooled Eggnog Filling between layers. Frost with Whipped Cream Frosting and garnish with nutmeg and red and green cherries. Refrigerate until serving time up to 24 hours. Makes 12 to 16 servings.

EGGNOG FILLING

3 tablespoons cornstarch
2 cups eggnog
½ teaspoon rum extract

Combine cornstarch with small amount of eggnog in stainless steel or glass saucepan. Blend until smooth. Blend in remaining eggnog and cook over simmering water until thickened and smooth. Add rum extract and cool.

WHIPPED CREAM FROSTING

2 cups heavy whipping cream
¼ cup sugar
Dash salt
1 teaspoon vanilla
½ teaspoon rum extract
1 teaspoon unflavored gelatin
2 tablespoons cold water

Combine whipping cream, sugar, salt and vanilla and rum extracts in mixing bowl, then chill. Whip until soft peaks form. Soften gelatin in cold water in cup. Place cup over hot water and gently stir gelatin until dissolved. Drizzle dissolved gelatin into whipped cream mixture and continue to beat until stiff.

IRISH WHISKEY CAKE

Leprechauns must be responsible for this modern-day cake mix version of whiskey cake.

1 (18.25-ounce) package yellow cake mix
1 (4-ounce) package instant chocolate pudding mix
¾ cup oil
¼ cup water
¼ cup Irish whiskey
¼ cup Irish cream liqueur
4 eggs

Combine cake mix, pudding mix, oil, water, whiskey, liqueur and eggs in bowl. Beat until smooth. Pour into greased and floured 10-inch Bundt pan or angel food cake pan. Bake at 350 degrees 40 to 50 minutes or until wood pick inserted near center comes out clean. Makes 10 servings.

UGLY DUCKLING PUDDING CAKE

General Foods named its own version of the "fruit cocktail cake" Ugly Duckling Pudding Cake, utilizing two of its mix products: a yellow cake mix and lemon-flavored gelatin.

1 package (2-layer size) yellow cake mix
1 package (4-serving size) lemon-flavored instant pudding
*   and pie filling mix*
1 (16-ounce) can fruit cocktail
1 cup flaked coconut
4 eggs
¼ cup oil
½ cup brown sugar, packed
½ cup chopped nuts, optional
Butter Glaze
Whipped topping

Blend together yellow cake mix, pudding mix, fruit cocktail with syrup, coconut, eggs and oil in large mixer bowl. Beat 4 minutes at medium speed of electric mixer. Pour into greased and floured 9 x 13-inch pan. Sprinkle with brown sugar and nuts. Bake at 325 degrees 45 minutes or until cake springs back when lightly pressed and pulls away from sides of pan. Do not underbake. Cool in pan 15 minutes. Spoon hot Butter Glaze over warm cake. Serve warm or cool with prepared whipped topping, if desired. Makes 1 (9 x 13-inch) cake, about 12 to 16 servings.

BUTTER GLAZE

½ cup butter or margarine
½ cup sugar
½ cup evaporated milk
1 ⅓ cups flaked coconut

Combine butter, sugar and milk in saucepan. Boil 2 minutes. Stir in coconut.

CHEESECAKES

AMARETTO CHOCOLATE CHEESECAKE

Readers can't seem to forget this cheesecake recipe from the Blue Lion in Jackson Hole, Wyoming.

> *6 (1-ounce) squares semisweet chocolate*
> *½ (8-ounce) package almond paste*
> *½ cup Amaretto*
> *3 (8-ounce) packages cream cheese, at room temperature*
> *½ cup sugar*
> *4 eggs*
> *½ cup whipping cream*
> *Chocolate Crumb Crust*

Melt chocolate. Cool slightly. Cut almond paste into small pieces and place in mixer bowl. Beat at low speed, gradually adding amaretto. Beat until well blended. Remove and set aside. In large bowl, beat cream cheese until smooth. Add sugar and beat until well blended. Beat in eggs. Add almond paste mixture. Add cooled chocolate and beat until blended. Add whipping cream. Mix until smooth. Fold in any leftover crumbs from Chocolate Crumb Crust. Pour into Chocolate Crumb Crust. Bake at 350 degrees about 45 minutes. Center of cake will be soft and solidify as it cools. Chill. Makes 10 to 12 servings.

> **CHOCOLATE CRUMB CRUST**
>
> *1 cup crushed coconut cookie bars (4 ounces)*
> *1 cup crumbled macaroons (4 ounces)*
> *5 tablespoons butter*
> *1 (1-ounce) square unsweetened chocolate*
> *2 tablespoons sugar*

Combine crumbs in food processor and blend until finely crumbled. Melt butter, chocolate and sugar in small saucepan. Add crumbs and mix well. Pat crumb mixture in bottom and around sides of buttered 9-inch springform pan.

❖

PUMPKIN CHEESECAKE

This wonderful pumpkin cheesecake recipe is requested every holiday season.

3 (8-ounce) packages cream cheese
1 cup sugar
4 eggs
1 (1-pound) can pumpkin with no spices added
2 ½ teaspoons ground ginger
1 tablespoon ground cinnamon
½ teaspoon ground nutmeg
¼ teaspoon ground cloves
⅓ cup brandy
Graham Cracker Crust

Cream together cream cheese and sugar until fluffy. Add eggs, 1 at time, beating well after each addition until smooth and creamy. Add pumpkin, ginger, cinnamon, nutmeg, cloves and brandy and mix until well blended. Turn cheese mixture into Graham Cracker Crust. Bake at 325 degrees 50 to 60 minutes, or until well puffed. Turn off heat and let cheesecake cool in oven. Makes 12 to 16 servings.

GRAHAM CRACKER CRUST

1 ½ cups graham cracker crumbs
¼ cup sugar
½ cup butter or margarine, melted

Combine crumbs, sugar and butter in bowl and mix until crumbs are moistened. Place crumb mixture into 10-inch springform pan and press 2 inches up sides of pan and on bottom. Bake at 350 degrees 20 minutes.

❖

LINDY'S TYPE NEW YORK CHEESECAKE

This cheesecake looks and tastes like the real thing from Lindy's in New York City.

> *1 cup sifted flour*
> *¼ cup sugar*
> *1 teaspoon grated lemon peel*
> *½ teaspoon vanilla*
> *1 egg yolk*
> *½ cup butter or margarine, softened*
> *Cheese Filling*

Combine flour, sugar, lemon peel and vanilla in bowl. Make well in center and add egg yolk and butter. Work with tips of fingers until dough forms ball and cleans sides of bowl.

Wrap dough in wax paper and chill about 1 hour. Roll ⅓ of dough between 2 pieces of floured wax paper to fit bottom of 9-inch springform pan. Remove sides from pan. Place dough on bottom of pan and trim dough by running rolling pin over edge. Bake at 400 degrees 8 to 10 minutes or until barely golden. Cool.

Roll remaining dough into 15 x 4-inch rectangle. Cut in half lengthwise. Carefully line sides of greased springform pan with dough strips, patching if necessary and pressing seams together.

Pour Cheese Filling into crust-lined pan and bake at 500 degrees 10 to 12 minutes. Reduce heat to 200 degrees and bake 1 hour longer. Let cool in draft-free area. Remove sides of pan and chill 12 to 24 hours. Makes 1 (9-inch) cheesecake, about 10 to 12 servings.

❖

CHEESE FILLING

5 (8-ounce) packages cream cheese, softened
1 ³/₄ cups sugar
3 tablespoons flour
¹/₄ teaspoon salt
1 teaspoon grated orange peel
¹/₂ teaspoon grated lemon peel
5 medium eggs
2 egg yolks
¹/₄ cup whipping cream

Beat cream cheese until fluffy. Combine sugar, flour, salt and orange and lemon peels. Stir into cream cheese until blended and mixture is smooth. Add eggs and egg yolks, 1 at time, blending well after each addition. Blend in cream.

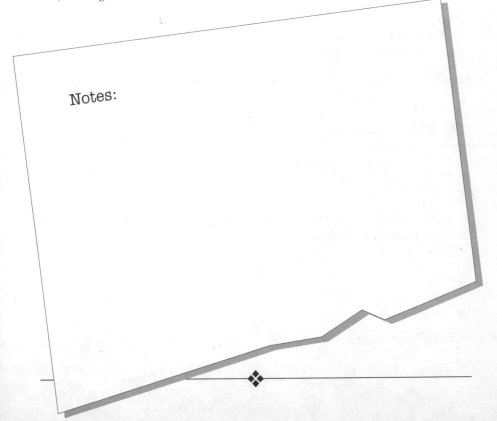

Notes:

HOLLYWOOD GRILLE CHOCOLATE CHEESECAKE

Robert's Hollywood Grille shared their terrific chocolate cheesecake.

1 pound semisweet chocolate pieces, melted
2 tablespoons butter
1 cup cold coffee
2 (8-ounce) packages cream cheese
1 (1-pound) carton sour cream
½ cup sugar
4 eggs
2 teaspoons vanilla
Graham Cracker Crust

Melt chocolate with butter and coffee until smooth. Beat cream cheese until soft. Beat in chocolate mixture, sour cream, sugar, eggs and vanilla. Turn into prepared Graham Cracker Crust. Bake at 300 degrees 2 hours or until wood pick inserted in center of cake comes out clean. Makes 6 to 8 servings.

GRAHAM CRACKER CRUST

1 cup crushed graham crackers
¼ cup sugar
¼ cup butter or margarine

Combine crushed graham crackers and sugar in bowl. Work in butter until crumbly. Press into greased 10-inch springform pan.

❖

CHOCOLATE

ACAPULCO PRINCESS' BLACK FOREST CAKE

A cruise line recipe came to the rescue for the fans of Black Forest Cake.

1/4 cup butter or margarine
1/3 cup plus 1 tablespoon sugar
2 eggs
1/2 cup plus 2 tablespoons milk
1 cup cake flour
1/2 teaspoon salt
2 tablespoons cocoa
1 teaspoon baking powder
1/2 teaspoon soda
1 tablespoon water
2 tablespoons kirsch or cherry liqueur
1/2 cup raspberry preserves
2 (17-ounce) cans dark sweet cherries, drained
3 1/2 to 4 cups sweetened whipped cream
Chocolate flakes

Cream butter and 1/3 cup sugar until light and fluffy. Beat in eggs, then milk. Beat until smooth.

Sift flour, salt, cocoa, baking powder and soda. Fold dry ingredients into egg mixture until blended. Pour into greased and floured 8-inch round cake pan. Bake at 350 degrees 30 minutes. Cool 10 minutes then remove from pan. Cool well.

Slice cake across twice to make 3 layers. Layers will be thin.

Mix together 1 tablespoon sugar, water and kirsch, then dampen top 2 layers (not bottom) with mixture. Spread all 3 layers with raspberry preserves. Cover each layer with cherries, then whipped cream. Place second and third layers atop bottom layer. Sprinkle top with chocolate flakes.

Chill until ready to serve. Makes 6 servings.

BROWNSTONE FRONT CAKE

Brownstone Front Cake has had many repeat performances since its first printing in 1965.

2 cups sifted flour
1 teaspoon baking soda
Dash salt
1 cup boiling water
2 squares unsweetened chocolate
½ cup butter or margarine
1¾ cups brown sugar, packed
2 eggs
½ cup sour cream
1 teaspoon vanilla
Chocolate Fudge Frosting

Sift together flour, baking soda and salt. Pour boiling water over chocolate and let stand until cool. Cream butter until soft, then gradually add brown sugar and continue to cream until light and fluffy. Beat in eggs.

Add flour mixture and sour cream alternately to butter mixture, beginning and ending with flour. Stir in chocolate mixture and vanilla. Turn batter into greased 9 x 5-inch loaf pan and bake at 325 degrees 50 to 60 minutes, or until cake tester inserted in center comes out clean. Cool in pan 5 minutes. Turn cake out onto rack. When completely cooled, frost top and sides with Chocolate Fudge Frosting or favorite frosting.

CHOCOLATE FUDGE FROSTING

1 ½ cups sugar
½ cup milk or half and half
1 tablespoon light corn syrup
1 tablespoon butter or margarine
2 (1-ounce) squares unsweetened chocolate, coarsely grated
1 teaspoon vanilla

Place sugar, milk, corn syrup, butter and chocolate in heavy saucepan with candy thermometer. Set over moderate heat and stir once or twice as chocolate melts. Boil without stirring until thermometer reaches 234 degrees or until a small amount of mixture dropped into cold water forms soft ball.

Remove from heat at once and cool without stirring to 120 degrees (lukewarm). Stir in vanilla and beat until thick and of spreading consistency. If too thick, add small amount of milk or half and half. If too thin, beat in small amount of sifted powdered sugar.

COCA-COLA CAKE

Coca-Cola Cake has been a conversation-piece cake for generations.

1 cup butter or margarine
1/4 cup cocoa
1 cup Coca-Cola
2 cups flour
2 cups sugar
1 teaspoon soda
1/2 cup buttermilk
2 eggs, beaten
1/2 teaspoon vanilla
1 1/2 cups miniature marshmallows
Frosting

In saucepan, heat butter, cocoa and Coca-Cola to boiling. Add flour, sugar and soda and mix gently. Stir in buttermilk, eggs, vanilla and marshmallows. Pour into greased 13x9-inch pan. Bake at 350 degrees 30 to 35 minutes. Cake can be frosted while warm. Decorate Frosting with tinted frosting, coconut and sugars, if desired. Makes 10 to 12 servings.

FROSTING

1/2 cup butter or margarine
1/4 cup cocoa
6 tablespoons Coca-Cola
1 cup miniature marshmallows
1 (1-pound) box powdered sugar, sifted
1/2 teaspoon vanilla
1 cup nuts

In saucepan, heat butter, cocoa and Coca-Cola to boiling. Add marshmallows, stirring until dissolved. Beat in sugar and vanilla. Stir in nuts. Spread over warm cake.

❖

ALMOST FLOUR-LESS CHOCOLATE CAKE

Serve a sliver of this delicious, dense chocolate cake after a light meal.

2 pounds bittersweet chocolate, melted
1 1/4 cups unsalted butter, at room temperature
8 eggs, separated
Dash salt
2 tablespoons sugar
2 tablespoons flour

Whisk chocolate and butter until blended. Whip egg yolks until pale yellow in color, about 5 minutes. Beat egg whites with salt, then add sugar, beating 5 seconds.

Fold chocolate into yolks, then fold into egg whites. Sift flour over mixture and fold in.

Butter bottom and sides of 10-inch baking pan. Pour chocolate mixture into pan. Bake at 425 degrees 15 minutes. Mixture will be soft. Cool completely before removing from pan. Makes 1 (10-inch) cake.

Notes:

DEVIL'S FOOD CAKE A LA 1930

The slightest dip in the economy brings out requests for Devil's Food Cake, straight out of the Depression Era.

½ cup shortening
1 ½ cups sugar
½ cup cocoa
¼ teaspoon salt
2 eggs
½ cup milk
2 teaspoons soda
2 cups flour
1 teaspoon vanilla
1 cup boiling water
Butter Frosting

Cream together shortening and sugar. Add cocoa, salt and eggs and mix well. Add milk in which soda has been dissolved. Stir in flour, vanilla and boiling water. Mix until smooth. Turn into 2 (9-inch) layer pans and bake at 350 degrees 30 to 35 minutes or until cakes spring back when lightly touched. Frost with Butter Frosting or White Mountain Frosting (see page 35). Makes 1 (9-inch) layer cake, or about 8 to 10 servings.

BUTTER FROSTING

1 (1-pound) box powdered sugar
⅓ cup butter or margarine, softened
¼ cup milk
1 teaspoon vanilla

Sift sugar and add butter, milk and vanilla. Beat 5 minutes or until smooth and creamy. Makes enough to frost 1 (2-layer) cake.

❖

HOT FUDGE PUDDING CAKE

Pudding cake recipes of this type have a cake-like topping over a soft pudding bottom.

1 cup flour
2 teaspoons baking powder
¼ teaspoon salt
¾ cup granulated sugar
6 tablespoons cocoa
½ cup milk
2 tablespoons shortening, melted
1 cup chopped nuts
1 cup brown sugar, packed
1¾ cups hot water

Sift flour, baking powder, salt, granulated sugar and 2 tablespoons cocoa into bowl. Stir in milk and melted shortening. Mix until smooth. Add nuts.

Spread batter in greased 8-inch-square pan. Mix brown sugar with remaining cocoa and sprinkle over top of batter. Pour hot water over entire batter.

Bake at 350 degrees 40 to 45 minutes. Cool slightly on wire rack. Cut into 1-inch squares. Invert squares on plate and dip sauce from pan over each. Makes 16 servings.

GERMAN'S CHOCOLATE CAKE

A close likeness to the recipe once printed on Baker's German's chocolate bar labels.

1 (¼-pound) package sweet cooking chocolate
½ cup boiling water
1 cup butter or margarine
2 cups sugar
4 eggs, separated
1 teaspoon vanilla
2 ½ cups flour, sifted
1 teaspoon soda
½ teaspoon salt
1 cup buttermilk
Coconut-Pecan Frosting

Melt chocolate in boiling water. Cool. In bowl, cream butter and sugar until light and fluffy. Add egg yolks, 1 at time, beating after each addition. Add vanilla and melted chocolate and mix until blended. Resift flour with soda and salt. Add sifted dry ingredients alternately with buttermilk, beating after each addition until batter is smooth. Stiffly beat egg whites and fold into batter.

Pour batter into 3 (8- or 9-inch) layer pans, lined on bottoms with wax paper. Bake at 350 degrees 35 to 50 minutes. Cool. Frost top and between layers with Coconut-Pecan Frosting. Makes 16 servings.

❖

COCONUT-PECAN FROSTING

1 cup evaporated milk
1 cup sugar
3 egg yolks
½ cup butter or margarine
1 teaspoon vanilla
1 (2½-ounce) can flaked coconut
1 cup chopped pecans

Combine milk, sugar, egg yolks, butter and vanilla in saucepan. Cook over medium heat 12 minutes, stirring constantly, until mixture thickens. Add coconut and pecans. Beat until cool and of spreading consistency.

LOMA LINDA CHOCOLATE-PRUNE CAKE

The cake developed at Loma Linda University cafeteria partially relies on the sugar naturally found in fruit.

¾ cup pitted prunes
¼ cup boiling water
⅔ cup oil
1 cup sugar
2 tablespoons cocoa powder
2 teaspoons ground cinnamon
1 teaspoon salt
1 teaspoon vanilla
2 eggs
1 cup buttermilk
2 ½ cups flour
1 ½ teaspoons baking soda
2 teaspoons baking powder
Chocolate Fudge Icing

Soak prunes in boiling water 30 minutes. Drain and set aside.

Combine oil, sugar, cocoa, cinnamon, salt and vanilla in bowl. Add eggs and beat well 2 minutes. Combine soaked prunes and buttermilk in blender container or food processor bowl and chop finely. Add to oil mixture with flour, baking soda and baking powder. Beat well.

Turn into greased and floured 13 x 9-inch baking pan or 2 (8-inch) round layer-cake pans. Bake at 350 degrees 30 minutes, or until wood pick inserted near center comes out clean. Cool and frost with Chocolate Fudge Icing. Makes 8 servings.

❖

CHOCOLATE FUDGE ICING

¼ cup water
¼ cup vegetable shortening
¼ cup white corn syrup
2 cups sifted powdered sugar
½ cup cocoa powder
¼ teaspoon salt
½ teaspoon vanilla

Bring water to boil. Remove from heat and beat in shortening and corn syrup. Add powdered sugar, cocoa, salt and vanilla. Beat to spreading consistency.

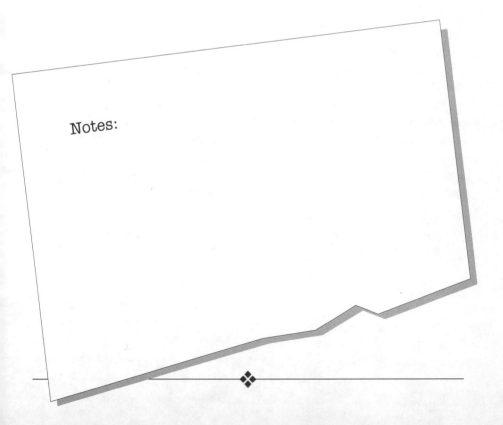

Notes:

ROYAL SONESTA DOUBLE CHOCOLATE CAKE

More than a few readers have characterized this Double Chocolate Cake from the Royal Sonesta Hotel in Cambridge, Mass., as "out of this world."

½ cup plus 2 tablespoons unsalted butter
1 cup sugar
½ cup cocoa powder
½ cup water
½ cup plus 2 tablespoons flour
½ teaspoon salt
1 ½ teaspoons baking powder
¾ teaspoon baking soda
4 large eggs
Orange-flavored liqueur
Ganache

Cream together butter and sugar until light and creamy. Stir in cocoa and water. Beat 7 minutes on electric mixer. Add flour, salt, baking powder and baking soda. Beat 2 minutes longer. Add eggs. Mix 5 minutes longer.

Pour batter into greased and floured 9-inch layer cake pan. Bake at 350 degrees 30 to 40 minutes or until cake center springs back when lightly touched. Invert onto wire rack to cool completely.

Split cake into 3 horizontal layers. Drizzle orange-flavored liqueur lightly over each layer. Frost layers with refrigerated Ganache. Pour remaining un-refrigerated Ganache over top layer to glaze. Makes 1 (3-layer) cake, about 12 servings.

GANACHE

18 ounces semisweet chocolate (squares or chips)
1 ½ cups whipping cream

Melt chocolate in top of double boiler over simmering water. Add whipping cream. Remove from heat. Remove 2 cups chocolate mixture and set aside. Refrigerate remaining chocolate mixture until thick and creamy. Use refrigerated portion for spreading between layers. Use un-refrigerated portion for glazing top layer of cake.

TUNNEL OF FUDGE CAKE

The original recipe using a cake mix won a $5,000 prize at the 17th Pillsbury Bake-Off contest in 1966, but has been since updated without cake mix when the cake mix was discontinued.

1 ¾ cups margarine or butter, softened
1 ¾ cups granulated sugar
6 eggs
2 cups powdered sugar
2 ¼ cups flour
¾ cup cocoa powder
2 cups chopped walnuts
Cocoa Glaze

Beat margarine and granulated sugar in large bowl until light and fluffy. Add eggs, 1 at time, beating well after each addition. Gradually add powdered sugar, blending well. By hand, stir in flour, cocoa and walnuts until well blended.

Spoon batter into greased and floured 12-cup fluted tube pan or 10-inch angel-food tube pan. Bake at 350 degrees 58 to 62 minutes. Cool in pan on cooling rack 1 hour. Invert onto serving plate. Cool completely.

Spoon Cocoa Glaze over top of cake, allowing some to run down sides. Makes 16 servings.

COCOA GLAZE

¾ cup powdered sugar
¼ cup cocoa powder
1 ½ to 2 tablespoons milk

Combine sugar, cocoa and milk in small bowl until well blended. Store tightly covered.

WACKY CAKE

Wacky Cake, so named because it has no eggs, has other names, too, such as cuckoo cake, crazy cake, cockeyed cake, punchy cake, black devil's cake and lickety-split cake.

1 ½ cups flour
1 cup sugar
¼ cup cocoa powder
1 teaspoon baking soda
½ teaspoon salt
1 cup water
6 tablespoons oil
1 tablespoon vinegar
1 teaspoon vanilla
2 tablespoons powdered sugar

Combine flour, sugar, cocoa, baking soda and salt. Add water, oil, vinegar and vanilla and stir just until batter is smooth and well-blended. Pour into greased and floured 9-inch layer cake pan or 8-inch square pan. Bake at 350 degrees 35 to 40 minutes or until cake tester inserted in center comes out clean. Cool. Dust with powdered sugar. Makes 9 servings.

COCONUT

BROWN DERBY DREAMY COCONUT CAKE

Brown Derby Dreamy Coconut Cake, a variation of the famous Grapefruit Cake, continues to gain fans long after the original Brown Derbies closed their doors.

1 ½ cups sifted cake flour
¾ cup sugar
1 ½ teaspoons baking powder
1 teaspoon salt
¼ cup water
¼ cup oil
3 eggs, separated
3 tablespoons grapefruit juice
½ teaspoon grated lemon zest
¼ teaspoon cream of tartar
White Mountain Frosting
Shredded coconut

Sift together flour, sugar, baking powder and salt into bowl. Make well in center and add water, oil, egg yolks, grapefruit juice and lemon zest. Beat until very smooth.

Beat egg whites with cream of tartar until stiff but not dry. Gradually add egg whites to batter and fold in gently until just blended. Do not stir.

Turn batter into ungreased 9-inch springform pan and bake at 350 degrees 30 minutes, or until top of cake springs back when lightly touched. Cool in pan on rack. Loosen edges of cake carefully and remove from pan. With serrated knife, cut cake crosswise to make 2 layers. Fill with part of White Mountain Frosting. Frost top and sides with remaining frosting. Sprinkle generously with coconut. Makes 8 to 12 servings.

Note: See page 42 for Grapefruit Cake.

WHITE MOUNTAIN FROSTING

2 cups sugar
¾ cup water
2 tablespoons light corn syrup
Dash salt
2 egg whites
¾ teaspoon vanilla

Combine sugar, water, corn syrup and salt in saucepan. Cook and stir over low heat until sugar dissolves. Cover saucepan 2 to 3 minutes to dissolve sugar crystals on sides of pan. Uncover and continue cooking to soft ball stage (236 degrees on candy thermometer). Remove from heat.

Beat egg whites until stiff but not dry. Add hot syrup in slow stream, beating constantly. Blend in vanilla and continue beating until frosting holds deep swirls.

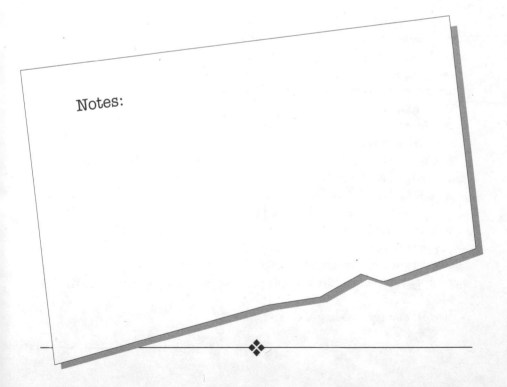

Notes:

PIÑA COLADA-WHITE COCONUT CAKE

Desserts with piña colada flavors soared to popularity in the '80s.

1 (1-pound 4-ounce) can crushed pineapple in heavy syrup
Water
½ teaspoon coconut extract
1 (18.5-ounce) box white cake mix
2 cups finely shredded fresh coconut
½ cup dark rum
2 egg yolks
1 cup powdered sugar
½ teaspoon vanilla
1 cup whipping cream, whipped until stiff
½ cup chopped pecans
Pecan halves, optional

Drain pineapple, reserving syrup. Chop pineapple very finely. Set aside. Add water to syrup to measure 1 ⅓ cups. Stir in coconut extract.

Prepare cake mix according to package directions, using pineapple syrup mixture in place of water called for in directions. Beat according to package directions. Fold in 1 cup coconut, ¼ cup rum and ¾ cup chopped pineapple. Set aside remaining coconut and pineapple.

Divide batter evenly between 2 greased and floured 9-inch cake pans. Bake at 350 degrees 30 to 35 minutes or until cakes are lightly browned and test done. Let cakes stand in pans on rack 5 minutes. Remove from pans to racks to cool.

With two-tine fork, pierce several holes in surface of cakes. Drizzle ¼ cup rum over cake layers while hot. Let cool.

For frosting, beat egg yolks. Beat in powdered sugar until light and fluffy. Stir in remaining ¼ cup rum and vanilla. Fold in whipped cream.

To assemble cake, spread reserved crushed pineapple on top of 1 cake layer. Spread with ½ cup whipped cream mixture and sprinkle with chopped pecans. Top with second cake layer. Frost cake with remaining whipped cream mixture. Sprinkle remaining coconut over top and sides of cake. Decorate with pecan halves. Chill until serving time. Makes 1 (2-layer) cake.

Note: See warning on the use of raw eggs, page 256.

FRUITCAKE

EVIE'S FRUITCAKE

Ever-popular Evie's Fruitcake from Mollie & Dollie, a mail order fruitcake company in Jacksboro, Texas, is made with sweetened condensed milk and no flour.

4 1/2 cups chopped pecans
3 1/2 cups chopped walnuts
2 pounds dates, chopped
1 pound candied cherries, cut up
1 pound candied pineapple, cut up
2 (14-ounce) cans sweetened condensed milk
2 (4-ounce) cans shredded coconut

Combine pecans, walnuts, dates, cherries (reserve few whole cherries for decoration), pineapple, condensed milk and coconut. Mix with hands. Turn into greased and floured 10-inch tube pan. Bake at 225 degrees about 1½ hours. (Cake is done when no milk oozes out when pressed with finger.)

Decorate with reserved cherries, if desired. Let cool. Turn out on foil and wrap snugly. Store in refrigerator or freezer about 1 month before serving. Makes 1 (10-inch) tube cake, about 12 servings.

LIGHT FRUITCAKE

You can allow fruitcake to mellow (and preserve it) by wrapping it in cheesecloth that has been doused in a high-proof alcohol of choice: rum, cognac, liqueurs or bourbon. Keep the cake in a cool dry place or in the refrigerator until ready to use.

1 cup golden raisins
½ pound candied citron
½ pound candied orange peel
1 pound candied cherries
¾ cup blanched almonds
4 cups sifted flour
1 tablespoon baking powder
1 ½ teaspoons salt
1 cup shortening
2 cups sugar
6 eggs
1 teaspoon lemon extract
1 cup orange juice

Chop raisins, citron, orange peel, cherries and almonds. Sift together flour, baking powder and salt. Sprinkle over fruit, mixing to coat well.

Cream shortening and sugar until fluffy. Beat in eggs, 1 at time. Add lemon extract, blending well. Add fruit mixture alternately with orange juice, mixing thoroughly. Pour into 3 greased, paper-lined 9 x 5-inch baking pans. Bake at 275 degrees 3½ hours or until knife inserted in center comes out clean. Makes 3 loaves (about 7 pounds fruitcake).

NO-BAKE FRUITCAKE

This fabulous fruitcake is easy to make because it requires absolutely no baking.

3/4 cup evaporated milk
1/3 cup apple juice
6 cups miniature marshmallows
4 3/4 cups crushed vanilla wafers
2 1/2 cups crushed gingersnaps
2 cups broken nuts
1 cup raisins
1 cup diced candied fruit
1 cup halved candied cherries

Pour milk and apple juice over marshmallows and let stand 3 hours. Stir occasionally. Combine crushed vanilla wafers, gingersnaps, nuts, raisins, fruit and cherries in large bowl. Add marshmallow mixture. Mix well. Pack into foil-lined 9 x 5-inch pan. Cover with foil. Refrigerate several days before slicing. Makes 1 loaf, about 12 servings.

FRUIT FLAVORED

PINEAPPLE UPSIDE-DOWN CAKE

We searched our files inside out for this old-fashioned upside-down cake.

1 (8 1/4-ounce) can sliced pineapple in syrup
3 tablespoons butter
1/4 cup brown sugar, packed
4 maraschino cherries, drained
3/4 cup flour
1/2 cup granulated sugar
3/4 teaspoon baking powder
1/4 teaspoon salt
1/8 teaspoon allspice
1/4 teaspoon grated orange zest
1/4 cup milk
1 egg

Drain pineapple, reserving 2 tablespoons syrup. Melt 2 tablespoons butter in 6-inch oven-proof skillet. Add brown sugar and stir until dissolved. Remove from heat. Place pineapple slices on top of sugar mixture. Fill center of each pineapple with 1 cherry.

Combine flour, granulated sugar, baking powder, salt and allspice in bowl. Blend orange zest with milk in separate bowl. Add remaining 1 tablespoon soft butter, egg and reserved 2 tablespoons syrup. Beat until blended. Add flour mixture and stir to make batter.

Pour batter over pineapple in skillet, being careful not to disturb slices. Bake at 350 degrees 45 minutes or until cake springs back when lightly touched. Let stand 5 minutes. Loosen edges and invert cake onto platter. Makes 6 servings.

❖

GULLIVER'S APPLE CRUMB CAKE

The sweet apple crumb cake is no longer on Gulliver's restaurant menu, but readers continue to request the recipe and it still makes a fine do-ahead holiday dessert for a party crowd.

> *6 large green apples, peeled, cored and sliced $\frac{1}{4}$-inch thick*
> *Grated zest of $\frac{1}{2}$ lemon*
> *$\frac{1}{2}$ (1-pound) box graham crackers, rolled into crumbs, about $4\frac{1}{3}$ cups*
> *1 cup brown sugar, packed*
> *1 teaspoon ground cinnamon*
> *Butter*
> *1 (10-ounce) jar currant jelly*
> *$\frac{1}{2}$ cup whipping cream, whipped*
> *$\frac{1}{2}$ cup toasted almond slices or 12 maraschino cherries*

Place apple slices in bowl with lemon zest. Combine cracker crumbs, brown sugar and cinnamon in separate bowl and mix well.

Soften $\frac{1}{3}$ cup butter at room temperature. Coat inside of 10-inch springform pan or parchment-lined cake pan with soft butter, then some of crumb mixture. Add $\frac{1}{2}$ cup layer of crumbs in bottom of pan. Pack half apple mixture firmly half full over crumbs in pan.

Whip currant jelly. Spread on thick layer of jelly over apples. Sprinkle over $\frac{3}{4}$ cup crumb mixture. Top with remaining apples. Make paste of remaining crumbs and $\frac{3}{4}$ cup butter. Cover apples with crumb mixture, packing down firmly. Bake at 300 degrees 2 hours. Cool. Cut into 12 portions. Decorate with whipped cream rosettes and almonds. Makes 12 servings.

Brown Derby Grapefruit Cake

Grapefruit Cake from the original Hollywood restaurant refuses to go out of style.

1 ½ cups sifted cake flour
¾ cup sugar
1 ½ teaspoons baking powder
1 teaspoon salt
¼ cup water
¼ cup oil
3 eggs, separated
3 tablespoons grapefruit juice
½ teaspoon grated lemon peel
¼ teaspoon cream of tartar
Cream Cheese Frosting
1 grapefruit, peeled and sectioned or 1 (1-pound) can grapefruit sections

Sift together flour, sugar, baking powder and salt into bowl. Make well in center and add water, oil, egg yolks, grapefruit juice and lemon peel. Beat until very smooth.

Beat egg whites with cream of tartar until stiff but not dry. Gradually pour egg yolk mixture over egg whites and fold in gently until just blended. Do not stir.

Turn batter into an ungreased 9-inch springform pan and bake at 350 degrees 30 minutes or until top springs back when touched lightly with finger. Invert onto rack and cool thoroughly.

Loosen edges of cake carefully and remove from pan. With a serrated knife cut cake crosswise to make two layers. Reserve a few sections for frosting.

Fill with part of Cream Cheese Frosting and grapefruit sections. Spread top and sides with frosting and decorate with additional fruit sections. Makes 1 (9-inch) tube cake, about 12 servings.

Note: See page 34 for coconut flavor variation.

CREAM CHEESE FROSTING

2 (3-ounce) packages cream cheese
2 teaspoons lemon juice
1 teaspoon grated lemon peel
¾ cup sifted powdered sugar
6 to 8 drops yellow food color, optional
Reserved grapefruit sections

Soften cream cheese at room temperature. Beat until fluffy. Add lemon juice and peel. Gradually blend in sugar and beat until well blended. Stir in food color. Crush enough grapefruit sections to measure 2 teaspoons and blend into frosting.

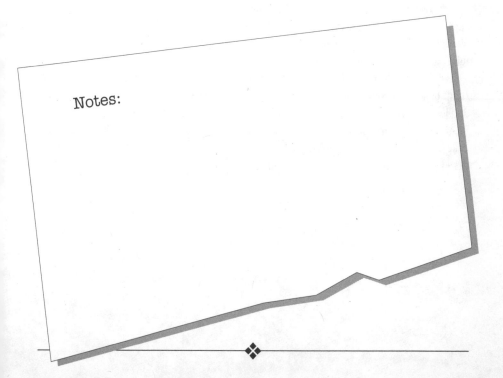

Notes:

NUT

BOURBON NUT CAKE

Get out the bourbon. You are going to have a very nice cake.

4 cups sifted flour
1 teaspoon baking powder
4 teaspoons ground nutmeg
1 cup butter or margarine
2 cups sugar
6 eggs
4 ounces bourbon, about
4 cups coarsely chopped pecans
1 pound dark raisins
$\frac{1}{2}$ pound candied cherries, sliced or chopped
Powdered sugar

Sift together flour, baking powder and nutmeg. Cream butter well, then gradually add sugar and continue to cream until fluffy. Beat in eggs, 1 at time. Add sifted dry ingredients alternately with bourbon. Stir in nuts, raisins and cherries. Turn batter into greased 10-inch tube pan lined on bottom with wax paper.

Bake at 300 degrees 2 hours, or until cake tester inserted near center comes out clean. If top begins to brown before cake is done, cover loosely with foil. Remove cake from oven and let stand 10 to 15 minutes, then turn out onto rack to cool completely.

When cool, sprinkle with additional bourbon and wrap. Use more bourbon if fragrant cake is desired. Let cake mellow 1 week or longer for best flavor. Sprinkle with sifted powdered sugar before slicing. Makes 1 (10-inch) cake, about 16 servings.

❖

UNITED AIRLINES MACADAMIA NUT CAKE

United Airlines Macadamia Nut Cake is actually a carrot cake.

1 ½ cups corn oil
2 cups sugar
3 eggs
2 cups flour
1 ½ cups shredded carrots
2 teaspoons baking soda
2 teaspoons salt
1 teaspoon ground cinnamon
1 teaspoon ground allspice
1 teaspoon vanilla
1 tablespoon cornstarch
¾ cup chopped macadamia nuts
Cream Cheese Icing

Combine corn oil, sugar, eggs, flour, carrots, baking soda, salt, cinnamon, allspice, vanilla, cornstarch and nuts. Mix until blended.

Turn batter into 13 x 9-inch pan and bake at 350 degrees 45 minutes to 1 hour. Let cool, then frost with Cream Cheese Icing. Makes 12 to 16 servings.

CREAM CHEESE ICING

1 (8-ounce) package cream cheese
¾ cup butter or margarine
2 cups powdered sugar
½ teaspoon vanilla
1 teaspoon lemon juice

Cream the cream cheese and butter with powdered sugar, vanilla and lemon juice until slightly fluffy. Spread on cooled cake.

❖

OTHER

BLUE-RIBBON PUMPKIN ROLL

The pumpkin roll was a blue-ribbon winner at the Los Angeles County Fair in 1985.

3 eggs
1 cup sugar
⅔ cup pumpkin puree
¾ cup flour
1 teaspoon baking powder
½ teaspoon salt
1 teaspoon ground ginger
2 teaspoons ground cinnamon
½ teaspoon ground nutmeg
1 cup finely chopped walnuts
Cream Cheese Filling

Beat eggs at high speed 5 minutes. Slowly beat in sugar. Stir in pumpkin.

Stir together flour, baking powder, salt, ginger, cinnamon and nutmeg. Fold into pumpkin mixture.

Spread mixture evenly in greased and floured paper-lined 15 x 10-inch jellyroll pan and sprinkle with nuts. Bake at 375 degrees 15 to 20 minutes.

Carefully loosen edges and turn out onto clean towel. Beginning at narrow end, roll up cake. Cool, unroll, fill with Cream Cheese Filling and re-roll. Slice to serve. Makes 1 (10-inch) pumpkin roll, about 10 to 12 servings.

CREAM CHEESE FILLING

1 (8-ounce) package cream cheese, softened
¼ cup butter or margarine, softened
½ teaspoon vanilla
1 cup powdered sugar

Beat together cream cheese, butter, vanilla and sugar until fluffy.

❖

BLUM'S COFFEE CRUNCH CAKE

Despite many imitations, reader taste for the original Blum's Coffee Crunch Cake has never waned since 1977, when the recipe from the famous San Francisco tearoom bakery was first printed.

1 ½ cups sugar
¼ cup strong coffee
¼ cup light corn syrup
1 tablespoon baking soda
1 cup whipping cream, whipped
1 (8-ounce) angel-food cake

Combine sugar, coffee and corn syrup in saucepan at least 5 inches deep. Bring mixture to boil and cook until it reaches 310 degrees on candy thermometer or reaches hard-crack stage (when small amount dropped into cold water breaks with brittle snap).

Press soda through sieve to remove lumps. Remove syrup from heat. Immediately add soda and stir vigorously just until mixture thickens and pulls away from sides of pan. (Mixture foams rapidly when soda is added. Do not destroy foam by beating excessively.)

Immediately pour foamy mass into ungreased 9-inch square metal pan (do not spread or stir). Let stand, without moving, until cool. When ready to garnish cake, knock out of pan and crush between sheets of wax paper with rolling pin to form coarse crumbs. Frost cake with whipped cream. Cover frosted cake generously and thoroughly with crushed topping. Refrigerate until ready to serve. Makes 6 servings.

CHURCH BUTTER POUNDCAKE

This old-fashioned butter poundcake, which was shared with us by members of the Apostolic Faith Assembly Church in Los Angeles, is one of the best we've tasted.

> *2 cups butter, softened*
> *1 (1-pound) package powdered sugar*
> *6 eggs*
> *3 cups cake flour*

Beat together butter and powdered sugar until light. Add eggs, one at a time, beating after each addition. Add flour, mixing only until smooth.

Spoon into greased 10-inch tube or fluted tube pan and bake at 325 degrees 1 hour 15 minutes. Cool before turning out onto wire rack to cool completely. Makes 1 (10-inch) cake, about 12 servings.

ITALIAN RUM CAKE *(Zuppa Inglese)*

A classic Italian rum cake.

> *6 egg yolks*
> *3 tablespoons sugar*
> *2 tablespoons honey*
> *¼ cup cream Sherry or Marsala*
> *1 (10-inch) sponge cake*
> *⅓ cup rum*
> *⅓ cup creme de cacao*
> *1 cup heavy whipping cream, whipped*
> *Chopped nuts*

Combine egg yolks, 2 tablespoons sugar and honey in top of double boiler. Beat with rotary beater until frothy and well blended. Beat in Sherry. Cook over hot but not boiling water, beating constantly until mixture starts to bubble. Immediately set double boiler top in pan of cold water to stop cooking. Continue beating until smooth and thick. Refrigerate custard until ready to use.

Cut cake into 3 layers. Place 1 layer on cake plate. In small bowl mix rum and creme de cacao. Spoon some over layer. Spread ⅓ of custard over layer, cover with another layer and repeat process twice, ending with custard over top layer. Chill several hours.

Just before serving, whip cream with remaining 1 tablespoon sugar until stiff. Spoon over torte. Sprinkle with nuts. Makes 10 to 12 servings.

POOR MAN'S CAKE

A cake made with no eggs and minimal butter became popular during the Great Depression.

1 tablespoon butter or margarine
½ cup sugar
½ cup dark corn syrup
2 cups flour
1 teaspoon ground cinnamon
½ teaspoon ground nutmeg
½ teaspoon ground cloves
1 teaspoon baking soda
⅔ cup cold coffee

Cream together butter and sugar in large bowl. Stir in corn syrup. Set aside.

Sift together flour, cinnamon, nutmeg and cloves. Dissolve soda in coffee. Add flour mixture and cold coffee mixture alternately to creamed mixture.

Pour into greased 13 x 9-inch pan. Bake at 350 degrees 45 to 50 minutes or until cake tests done. Makes 10 to 12 servings.

Notes:

KATHY'S BROADWAY CARROT CAKE

Readers have used the Broadway Department store's recipe for carrot cake for more than a decade.

3 cups grated carrots (4 large carrots)
2 cups sugar
2 cups flour
4 eggs
1 ½ cups oil
1 (8-ounce) package cream cheese, softened
2 teaspoons baking soda
1 teaspoon salt
1 teaspoon ground cinnamon
1 teaspoon vanilla
1 cup chopped nuts
Cream Cheese Icing

Beat together carrots, sugar, flour, eggs, oil and cream cheese. Add baking soda, salt, cinnamon, vanilla and nuts to mixture and mix well. Pour batter into greased and floured 13 x 9-inch pan and bake at 350 degrees 55 minutes. Cool and frost with Cream Cheese Icing.

CREAM CHEESE ICING

¼ cup butter or margarine
1 (8-ounce) package cream cheese, softened
1 pound powdered sugar
2 tablespoons milk
1 teaspoon vanilla

Cream together butter and cream cheese. Add powdered sugar, milk and vanilla and beat until smooth. Spread on cooled cake.

OLD-FASHIONED PEPPERMINT CAKE

If you have candy canes left over from Christmas, a pretty pink peppermint Easter cake will serve you well.

3 cups sifted flour
1 tablespoon baking powder
1 teaspoon salt
¾ cup butter or margarine
1 ½ cups sugar
¾ cup milk
½ cup water
1 teaspoon vanilla
3 egg whites
Pink Peppermint Frosting

Sift together flour, baking powder and salt. Cream together butter and sugar until light and fluffy. Combine milk, water and vanilla. Add flour mixture to creamed mixture alternately with milk mixture, beating after each addition.

Beat egg whites until stiff but not dry. Fold egg whites into batter. Turn into 2 greased paper-lined 9-inch round pans. Bake at 350 degrees 35 to 40 minutes or until cake tester inserted in center comes out clean. Cool 10 minutes, then turn onto wire rack to cool completely. Frost with Pink Peppermint Frosting. Makes 1 (9-inch) layer cake, about 8 to 10 servings.

PINK PEPPERMINT FROSTING

2 egg whites
1/4 teaspoon cream of tartar
1/4 teaspoon lemon extract
1/4 teaspoon peppermint extract
Dash salt
1 pound package powdered sugar
1/3 cup butter or margarine
Few drops red food color
1/2 cup crushed peppermint candy

Combine egg whites, cream of tartar, lemon and peppermint extracts and salt. Beat at high speed on mixer until fairly stiff.

Gradually add sugar, 1 cup at time. Beat until smooth, scraping bowl often. Add butter and food color, beating until well blended. Stir in crushed peppermint candy. Makes enough to frost 2 (9-inch) layers.

Note: For green mint frosting, use green food color and omit crushed peppermint candy
Note: See warning on the use of raw eggs, page 256.

Notes:

POPPY SEED CAKE

The darkness of Poppy Seed Cake depends on the quantity of seeds used.

1 cup poppy seeds
¼ cup water
⅓ cup honey
1 cup butter or margarine
1 ½ cups sugar
4 eggs, separated
1 cup sour cream
1 teaspoon vanilla
2 ½ cups sifted flour
1 teaspoon soda
1 teaspoon salt
Powdered sugar

Combine poppy seeds, water and honey in small saucepan and cook over medium heat 5 to 7 minutes. Cool.

Cream together butter and sugar until light and fluffy. Stir in poppy seed mixture. Add egg yolks 1 at time, beating well after each addition. Stir in sour cream and vanilla. Sift together flour, soda and salt. Gradually add dry ingredients to poppy seed mixture, beating well after each addition. Beat egg whites until stiff and fold into batter.

Turn batter into greased and floured 9-inch tube pan and bake at 350 degrees 1 hour and 15 minutes, or until cake springs back when lightly touched with finger. Cool in pan 5 minutes, then remove cake to rack and cool. Before serving dust with powdered sugar. Makes 10 servings.

Note: Use more poppy seeds if darker cake is desired.

TEACAKES

Old-fashioned tea cakes were popular in the South many years ago, but appear in bakeries throughout the country today.

½ cup brown sugar, packed
¼ cup granulated sugar
½ teaspoon salt
2 tablespoons oil
1 egg
¾ cup cake flour
½ teaspoon baking powder
¼ teaspoon baking soda
½ cup buttermilk
3 tablespoons fine-chopped pecans
Cream Icing

Mix together sugars, salt and oil. Add egg and beat until smooth. Sift together cake flour, baking powder and soda. Stir in half of buttermilk and mix until blended, then add remaining buttermilk and beat until smooth.

Divide pecans among 8 greased muffin cups. Add batter, filling ⅔ full. Bake at 350 degrees until golden, about 20 to 30 minutes. Remove from pans onto clean cloth. Cool. Dip nut side into Cream Icing and place on rack to set. Icing will be thick when dry. Makes 8 cakes.

CREAM ICING

½ cup brown sugar, packed
½ teaspoon butter
2 tablespoons whipping cream or half and half

Combine sugar, butter and cream in saucepan. Bring to boil. Cool only slightly before dipping, or keep hot until ready to dip so syrup does not harden.

BOSTON CREAM PIE

Boston Cream Pie, actually a layered sponge cake with custard and chocolate topping, was at its peak of popularity during the first half of the century when most every coffee shop or restaurant on the East Coast served it.

2 (9-inch) layers butter cake, sponge cake
  or cake made from yellow cake mix
Vanilla Cream Filling, double cream (Devonshire)
  or 1 ½ cups sweetened whipped cream
Chocolate Glaze

Sandwich cake layers together with Vanilla Cream Filling or other desired filling. Spread Chocolate Glaze on top and let stand until glaze hardens. Store in refrigerator. Makes 6-8 servings.

VANILLA CREAM FILLING

2 tablespoons cornstarch
⅓ cup sugar
¾ cup milk
1 egg yolk
1 teaspoon vanilla

Blend cornstarch, sugar and milk in small saucepan and heat, stirring constantly, over moderate heat until mixture boils and thickens. Boil and stir ½ minute longer. Remove from heat.

Beat small amount of hot mixture (about ¼ cup) into egg yolk, then return to pan gradually, beating constantly. Mix in vanilla and cool to room temperature, beating occasionally.

❖

CHOCOLATE GLAZE

2 (1-ounce) squares unsweetened chocolate
1 teaspoon butter or margarine
1 cup sifted powdered sugar
3 tablespoons warm water

Melt chocolate and butter in top of double boiler over simmering water. Stir to blend well. Set top of double boiler on damp cloth, add ½ cup powdered sugar and 1 tablespoon water. Beat until smooth. Add remaining sugar and water and beat until glossy.

COOKIES

C ookies are near the top when it comes to requests. You'll find most of the ones you'd think to request, plus a few you might have been overlooked. Be sure to try *World's Best Sugar Cookies*, *Thumbprints* and *London Strips*, some of the most frequently requested cookie recipes. Check in our previous book, "Dear S.O.S.," for others favorites not present here.

Dear S.O.S.:
    You gave the wrong recipe to reader "Terry" who was looking for the "best sugar cookies ever." This is the one she wants and it's called World's Best Sugar Cookies.
        – Joy

Dear Joy:
    How nice of you to straighten us out with the correct recipe and title for these great sugar cookies.

BALL

POTATO CHIP COOKIES

This recipe dates back to 1975 when it was first printed after appearing on potato chip packages.

> *1 cup butter or margarine*
> *Sugar*
> *1 teaspoon vanilla*
> *½ cup crushed potato chips*
> *½ cup chopped nuts*
> *2 cups flour*

Cream butter and ½ cup sugar. Add vanilla, potato chips, nuts and flour and mix well. Form into small balls and place on ungreased baking sheets. Dip glass in sugar and flatten cookies. Bake at 350 degrees 16 to 18 minutes. Makes 80 cookies.

❖

PEANUT BUTTER COOKIES

These cholesterol-free cookies were a My Best Recipe winner back in 1969.

1 ½ cups peanut butter
1 cup powdered sugar
2 unbeaten egg whites

Combine peanut butter and sugar and blend well. Add egg whites and mix thoroughly. Roll into walnut-size balls and place on ungreased baking sheets. Flatten with fork. Bake at 375 degrees 10 to 12 minutes. Cool slightly before removing from pan. Makes 3 dozen.

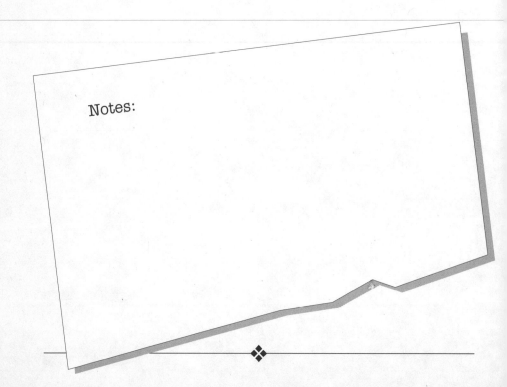

Notes:

THUMBPRINTS

Thumbprints have a way of leaving their mark on readers.

3 cups flour
½ teaspoon nutmeg
1 cup brown sugar, packed
1 cup plain coconut or raisin natural-type cereal
1 cup butter or margarine, softened
1 (5.3-ounce) can evaporated milk
½ teaspoon almond extract
1 ½ cups shredded coconut
Any flavor red jelly

Combine flour, nutmeg, sugar and coconut. Work in butter until crumbly. Gradually stir in milk and almond extract until well blended. Refrigerate until firm enough to roll into balls. Form 1½-inch balls and roll each in coconut.

Place on greased baking sheets. Press with thumb to make hollow in center. Bake at 375 degrees 10 to 12 minutes, or until lightly browned on bottom. Remove from baking sheets to wire rack. Cool completely, then store in airtight containers. When ready to serve, place spoonful of jelly in center. Makes about 5 dozen.

BAR

CRANBERRY CHEWS

Cranberry Chews is a prize-winning recipe from a reader.

4 eggs
2 cups sugar
Juice of 1 lemon
½ teaspoon lemon flavoring
½ teaspoon almond extract
3 cups flour
1 tablespoon baking powder
½ teaspoon salt
1½ cups chopped pecans
1 (1-pound) can jellied cranberry sauce, diced in ¼-inch cubes
Powdered Sugar Frosting

Beat eggs. Gradually add sugar and continue beating until creamy. Add lemon juice, lemon flavoring and almond extract. Sift flour, baking powder and salt together and stir into egg-sugar mixture. Fold in pecans and cranberry sauce. Mix lightly.

Divide batter between 2 greased (15 x 10-inch) shallow pans. Bake at 350 degrees 30 minutes. Frost with Powdered Sugar Frosting and cut in squares while still warm. Makes 6 to 7 dozen.

POWDERED SUGAR FROSTING

3 cups powdered sugar
6 to 8 tablespoons milk
¼ cup butter, softened
1 teaspoon vanilla

Mix together powdered sugar, milk, butter and vanilla until smooth and creamy.

❖

HAPPY TRAILS PECAN BARS

This relative newcomer from Happy Trails Catering in Pasadena, California, makes a great treat packed in a school lunch.

2 cups flour
½ cup powdered sugar
1 cup unsalted butter, cut into ½-inch cubes
2 ½ cups pecans
Pecan Topping

Combine flour and sugar in food processor. Add butter and pulse on and off 6 to 8 times or until mixture is crumbly. Pat dough into 11 x 7-inch baking pan. Bake at 400 degrees 20 minutes or until light golden-brown.

Sprinkle with pecans and pour Pecan Topping in thin stream over pecans, covering entire surface. Bake at 350 degrees 25 to 30 minutes. Cut into bars. Makes about 24 bars.

PECAN TOPPING

1 egg
1 cup brown sugar, packed
2 tablespoons butter, melted
½ teaspoon vanilla
½ cup corn syrup

Mix egg, brown sugar, butter, vanilla and corn syrup in bowl.

❖

LONDON STRIPS

An old favorite, London Strips are layered with strawberry jam and meringue.

2 ½ cups flour
5 eggs, separated
1 cup plus 6 tablespoons sugar
1 cup unsalted butter
1 tablespoon vanilla
Strawberry jam
1 tablespoon bourbon or vanilla extract
3 cups walnuts, finely chopped
Powdered sugar

In bowl, mix flour, egg yolks, 6 tablespoons sugar, butter and vanilla, blending thoroughly.

Spread dough on 16 x 11-inch pan and flatten. Cover liberally with jam. In bowl beat egg whites until stiff, gradually beating in 1 cup sugar and bourbon. Fold in nuts and spread mixture over dough.

Bake at 350 degrees about 40 minutes. Sprinkle with powdered sugar, then cut into strips when cool. Makes 3 to 4 dozen strips.

❖

MISTO LEMON BARS

Misto Bakery and Cafe in Torrance, California, came through with this popular recipe.

2 ¼ cups sifted flour
½ cup sifted powdered sugar
1 cup butter
8 eggs
3 ½ cups granulated sugar
1 cup lemon juice
4 teaspoons grated lemon zest
1 teaspoon baking powder
1 tablespoon unsifted flour

Sift together sifted flour and powdered sugar. Cut in butter until mixture resembles crumbs.

Pat in bottom of 13 x 9-inch baking pan. Bake at 350 degrees until golden brown.

Beat eggs with granulated sugar and stir in lemon juice, zest, baking powder and unsifted flour. Mix well. Pour over crust. Bake at 350 degrees 45 minutes. Cut into 32 (1½ x 2-inch) bars. Makes about 32 bars.

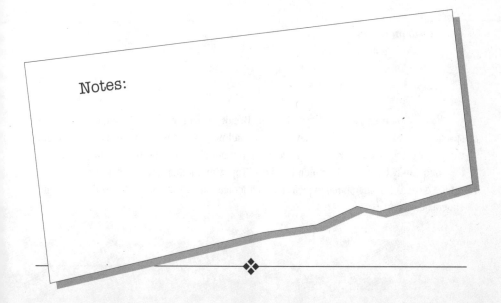

Notes:

PEANUT BUTTER-GRANOLA BARS

Be sure to let the bars stand until firm before cutting.

1 (6-ounce) package semisweet chocolate pieces
1 (6-ounce) package butterscotch pieces
$\frac{1}{2}$ cup peanut butter
1 cup miniature marshmallows
5 cups oven-toasted rice cereal
Butter

Combine chocolate and butterscotch pieces with peanut butter in heavy 3-quart saucepan. Cook and stir over low heat until blended. Remove from heat. Add marshmallows and cereal, stirring until both are well coated.

Press mixture into buttered 13 x 9-inch pan, then let stand in cool place until firm. Cut into 2x1-inch bars. Makes 48 bars.

S'MORES

There is more to S'Mores than meets the eye.

Graham crackers
Chocolate candy bars
Marshmallows

Place graham crackers in layer in pan. Break up candy bars into small pieces and spread over layer of crackers. Skewer marshmallows on wet wood or metal skewers and toast over dying coals or flame. When toasted, but not charred, carefully slip off marshmallow onto candy bar-layered graham crackers. Top with another layer graham crackers and squish closed. Hot marshmallow will melt chocolate slightly, or bake at 350 degrees until chocolate melts.

MARIE'S BROWNIES

This brownie recipe is another reader favorite.

½ cup butter or margarine
4 squares unsweetened chocolate
4 eggs
2 teaspoons vanilla
2 cups sugar
1 cup sifted flour
1 cup coarsely chopped walnuts
Powdered sugar or chocolate frosting, optional

Combine butter and chocolate. Place over low heat and melt. Set aside. Beat eggs and vanilla in mixing bowl. Gradually add sugar, beating well. Stir in chocolate mixture, then flour and nuts.

Turn batter into greased 9-inch-square pan and bake at 350 degrees 30 to 35 minutes. Cool before cutting into bars. Sprinkle with powdered sugar or spread with prepared chocolate frosting, if desired. Makes 4 ½ dozen (1 x 1½-inch) bars.

MARSHMALLOW BARS

Children of all ages love to make these no-bake cookies.

½ cup butter or margarine
1 ½ pounds marshmallows
1 (6-ounce) box crisp rice cereal
1 (6-ounce) package semisweet chocolate pieces
½ cup chopped nuts

Melt butter in large saucepan. Add marshmallows and stir over low heat until very soft but still lumpy. Add rice cereal and mix thoroughly, then stir in chocolate pieces and nuts. Wet hands and press mixture firmly into greased 15 x 11-inch jelly roll pan. Cool until firm, then cut into squares. Makes about 4 dozen squares.

SOME CRUST DARK-CHOCOLATE BROWNIES

A reader described the brownies from Some Crust Bakery in Claremont as a "dark-chocolate lover's dream."

1 cup unsalted butter
1 cup sugar
4 eggs
½ cup flour
½ cup cocoa
½ teaspoon salt
½ teaspoon baking powder
½ cup tiny chocolate chips
½ cup toasted chopped walnuts

Cream butter and sugar until fluffy. Continue to beat while adding eggs, 1 at time, until mixture is pale in color. Set aside.

Sift flour and cocoa into separate bowl. Add salt and baking powder. Mix until dry ingredients are well combined. Gradually add dry ingredients to butter mixture, beating only enough to mix thoroughly. Fold in chocolate chips and nuts.

Pour into well-buttered 13 x 9-inch baking pan. Bake at 350 degrees until brownies are firm, about 25 minutes. Cool, then cut into squares. Makes 24 brownies.

❖

Chewie Brownies

Chewie Brownies make use of a devil's-food cake mix, so they are easier than one would expect.

> 1 pound caramels
> ⅔ cup evaporated milk
> ¾ cup butter or margarine, softened
> 1 (18.5-ounce) package devil's-food cake mix
> 1 cup chopped pecans
> 1 (6-ounce) package semisweet chocolate pieces
> 1 cup pecan halves or chopped nuts

Combine caramels and ⅓ cup evaporated milk in top of double boiler. Melt over simmering water, stirring frequently. Keep melted.

Cream butter in large bowl until light and smooth. Beat in cake mix and remaining ⅓ cup evaporated milk. Stir in chopped pecans and chocolate pieces. Turn into greased 13 x 9-inch baking pan. Bake at 350 degrees 35 to 45 minutes or until cake tests done. Cool slightly.

Top with pecan halves and drizzle on caramel mixture. Or spread with caramel mixture and top with halved or chopped nuts. Makes about 15 servings.

VACUUM CLEANER COOKIES *(Neiman-Marcus Squares)*

This recipe came from reader Connie Hankins, who says that the popular cookies are also known by the slightly more upscale name: Neiman-Marcus Squares.

> *½ cup margarine (not butter), melted*
> *1 (18.25-ounce) box yellow cake mix*
> *3 eggs*
> *1 (8-ounce) package cream cheese, softened*
> *1 (1-pound) box powdered sugar*
> *½ cup flaked coconut*
> *½ cup chopped walnuts or pecans*

Combine margarine, cake mix and 1 egg in mixing bowl. Stir together until dry ingredients are moistened. Pat mixture into bottom of well-greased 15 x 10-inch jellyroll pan.

Beat remaining 2 eggs lightly, then beat in cream cheese and powdered sugar. Stir in coconut and nuts. Pour over mixture in jellyroll pan, spreading evenly.

Bake at 325 degrees 45 to 50 minutes or until golden brown. Cool pan on wire rack to room temperature. Cut into bars. Makes about 4 dozen bars.

Note: Use plain cake mix, not mix with pudding added.

❖

CUTOUT

BASIC REFRIGERATOR (ICE BOX) COOKIES

The name, ice box cookies, has been converted to refrigerator cookies but the recipe is the same.

2 ¾ cups flour
¾ teaspoon salt
½ teaspoon baking powder
½ teaspoon soda
1 cup butter
1 cup sugar
2 eggs
1 teaspoon vanilla

Sift together flour, salt, baking powder and soda. In bowl cream butter and sugar until light and fluffy. Beat in eggs 1 at a time. Add vanilla. Gradually add dry ingredients to creamed mixture, mixing well after each addition.

Shape dough into 1½- to 2-inch rolls. Wrap rolls in foil. Chill at least 3 hours or overnight in refrigerator. Cut into slices ⅛ to ¼ inch thick. Bake on ungreased baking sheets at 375 degrees 10 to 12 minutes. Makes about 3 dozen.

❖

COCONUT WASHBOARDS

We located the recipe for this popular old-fashioned favorite in a booklet published by General Foods Corp.

2 cups flour
³⁄₄ teaspoon baking powder
¹⁄₄ teaspoon ground cinnamon
¹⁄₄ teaspoon ground nutmeg
¹⁄₈ teaspoon salt
³⁄₄ cup butter
1 cup brown sugar, packed
1 egg
1 teaspoon vanilla extract
¹⁄₂ teaspoon almond extract
1 ¹⁄₃ cups flaked coconut

Mix flour with baking powder, cinnamon, nutmeg and salt in mixing bowl.

Cream butter in separate bowl. Gradually add brown sugar, beating until light and fluffy. Add egg and vanilla and almond extracts. Beat well. Add flour mixture, blending well. Stir in coconut.

Divide dough into 2 parts. Spread or pat each half into 10 x 9-inch rectangle. Chill, if necessary, until dough is easily handled. Cut each rectangle into 4 strips lengthwise. Cut each strip into 10 pieces.

Place about 2 inches apart on ungreased baking sheet. Using a floured fork, gently press ridges into cookies. Bake at 375 degrees until golden brown, about 8 to 10 minutes. Makes about 6 ½ dozen.

DUTCH NUTMEG COOKIES

Readers never seem to forget these classic cookies.

1 cup butter or margarine
¼ teaspoon baking soda
¼ teaspoon salt
¼ teaspoon ground cloves
½ teaspoon ground nutmeg
1 teaspoon ground cinnamon
1 cup sugar
½ cup chopped nuts
2 cups sifted flour
¼ cup sour cream

Cream butter with baking soda, salt, cloves, nutmeg and cinnamon until fluffy. Gradually add sugar, beating until fluffy. Stir in nuts. Add flour alternately with sour cream. Mix well.

Shape into 12 x 2-inch roll. Wrap in foil or wax paper and chill several hours or overnight. Cut into ⅛-inch slices. Bake at 375 degrees 25 minutes. Cool on wire racks. Makes 4 dozen.

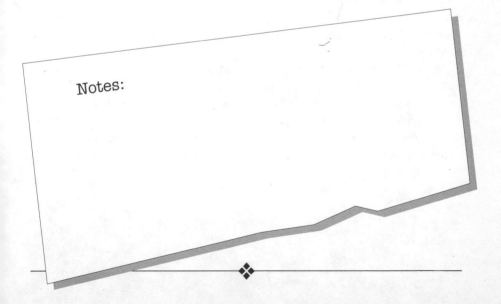

Notes:

MORAVIAN COOKIES

True Moravian Cookies are difficult to roll paper-thin using home methods. The suggestion is to shape the dough into a roll, freeze and slice paper-thin. Included are methods for both slicing and rolling.

1/3 cup light molasses
1/4 cup soft butter or margarine
2 tablespoons sugar
1 1/4 cups sifted flour
1/2 teaspoon salt
1/2 teaspoon baking soda
1/4 teaspoon ground cinnamon
1/4 teaspoon ground ginger
1/4 teaspoon ground cloves

Blend together molasses, butter and sugar. Sift together flour, salt, baking soda, cinnamon, ginger and cloves. Blend dry ingredients into butter mixture and mix well. Cover with plastic wrap and refrigerate at least 2 hours. (Dough may be refrigerated several days).

To slice paper-thin, shape dough into roll about 2 inches in diameter, then freeze. Slice paper-thin with sharp knife. Place on greased baking sheet and bake at 375 degrees 5 to 6 minutes or until only slightly browned. Remove from oven and cool 3 minutes. Remove cookies from pan onto cooling rack or paper towels. When cool, store in tightly covered container.

Or, to roll cookies, stretch pastry cloth over large cutting board. Sprinkle cloth generously with flour. Rub flour into cloth with hands and brush off excess. Remove about 1/3 of dough from refrigerator at a time. Roll as thin as possible. Use only as much flour as necessary to keep dough from sticking to pin. Cut with round, fluted-edged pastry cutter or various cookie cutters. Place on greased baking sheet and bake at 375 degrees 5 to 6 minutes or until only slightly browned. Cool on rack, then store in tightly covered container. Makes about 6 dozen.

❖

ZWIEBACK TOAST

These old-fashioned toast cookies were originally made with compressed yeast, a fresh yeast, used before World War II, which required refrigeration (or storing in the ice box). Dry yeast was developed during the war and is, by far, the most widely available form of yeast sold today. Here's a recipe for Zwieback, whose yeast content we altered for our readers.

> *1 package dry yeast*
> *½ cup lukewarm water*
> *2 cups scalded milk, cooled*
> *9 cups unbleached flour*
> *¾ cup butter*
> *½ cup sugar*
> *½ teaspoon ground cinnamon*
> *3 eggs, beaten*

Dissolve yeast in lukewarm water. Add cooled milk. Stir in about 3 cups flour and beat until thoroughly mixed. Cover with clean cloth and let rise until light, about 60 minutes.

Add butter, sugar mixed with cinnamon, eggs and enough flour to make dough. Knead until soft, elastic and smooth. Cover and let rise until doubled.

Shape into long narrow loaves, about 3 inches in diameter. Place on greased baking sheets and bake at 350 degrees 50 minutes or until golden. Cool on wire racks. Cut into slices about ½-inch thick and brown in oven or dry in slow oven without browning. Makes 60 (½-inch) thick slices.

Note: For thicker toast, cut into 1-inch slices.

DROP

ANISE COOKIES

It's an easy and, yes, excellent cookie with tea or champagne.

> 4 eggs
> 1 $1/4$ cup sugar
> 3 cups sifted flour
> 1 $1/2$ tablespoons anise seeds, lightly crushed

Beat eggs with sugar about 10 minutes with electric mixer. Mixture should be pale yellow and thick enough to ribbon. Sift flour again and add to egg batter, little at time, mixing well after each addition. Mix in anise seeds.

Drop dough by teaspoons 1 inch apart onto greased baking sheet. Let dry uncovered at room temperature overnight. Bake at 300 degrees until golden, about 10 minutes. Makes 7 dozen.

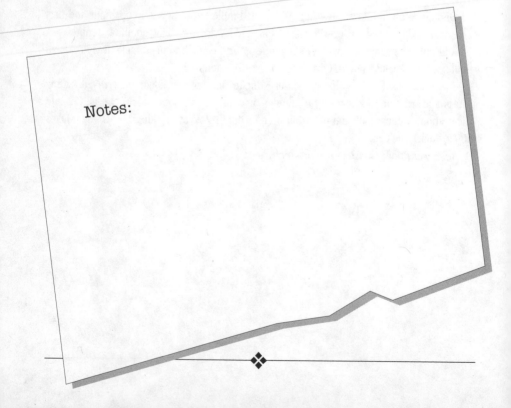

Notes:

❖

CORNMEAL COOKIES

It's always time for a repeat performance, when it comes to cornmeal cookies.

³/₄ cup butter or margarine
³/₄ cup sugar
1 egg
1 teaspoon baking powder
1 ½ cups flour
¼ teaspoon salt
½ cup cornmeal
½ teaspoon ground nutmeg, optional
½ cup raisins, optional

Cream butter and sugar in large bowl. Add egg and beat well. Add baking powder, flour, salt, cornmeal, nutmeg and raisins and mix well. Drop by teaspoons onto greased baking pan. Bake at 350 degrees about 15 minutes, until lightly browned on top. Makes about 3 dozen.

GREAT PUMPKIN COOKIES

This recipe for pumpkin cookies helps use up Halloween pumpkins in a delicious way.

2 cups flour
1 cup oats
1 teaspoon baking soda
1 teaspoon ground cinnamon
½ teaspoon salt
1 cup butter or margarine, softened
1 cup brown sugar, packed
1 cup granulated sugar
1 egg
1 teaspoon vanilla
1 cup mashed canned or cooked pumpkin
1 cup semisweet chocolate pieces
Icing of choice or peanut butter
Assorted candies, raisins or nuts

Combine flour, oats, baking soda, cinnamon and salt. Set aside.

Cream butter. Gradually add brown and granulated sugars, beating until light and fluffy. Add egg and vanilla, mixing well.

Alternately add dry ingredients and pumpkin, mixing well after each addition. Stir in chocolate pieces.

For each cookie, drop ¼ cup dough onto lightly greased baking sheet. Spread into pumpkin shape using thin metal spatula. Add bit more dough to form stems.

Bake at 350 degrees 20 to 25 minutes until cookies are firm and lightly browned. Remove from baking sheets and cool on wire racks. Decorate using icing or peanut butter to affix assorted candies, raisins or nuts. Makes about 20 cookies.

Note: One cup raisins may be substituted for chocolate pieces.

HARD CHOCOLATE CHIP COOKIES

This is a good chocolate chip cookie, if you like a famous brand.

1 cup butter
2 eggs
¾ cup brown sugar, packed
¾ cup granulated sugar
1 teaspoon baking powder
½ teaspoon baking soda
2 ¼ cups flour
2 cups semisweet chocolate pieces
1 cup raisins

Cream together butter, eggs and sugars until light and fluffy. Sift together baking powder, baking soda and flour. Stir into creamed mixture until well blended. Fold in chocolate and raisins. Drop by teaspoons onto greased baking sheets and bake at 350 degrees 7 minutes. Makes about 8 dozen.

❖

HARRIS RANCH OATMEAL-RAISIN COOKIES

Oatmeal-raisin cookies from the Harris Ranch in Coalinga rely on pastry flour available at health food stores and some markets for proper texture.

¾ cup butter
1 ½ cups brown sugar, packed
1 teaspoon vanilla
Dash salt
1 cup pastry flour
2 cups oats
1 teaspoon baking powder
2 eggs
⅓ cup walnuts
1 cup raisins

Cream butter, brown sugar, vanilla and salt in mixer bowl. In separate bowl mix flour, oats and baking powder. Add to butter mixture and mix well. Add eggs, walnuts and raisins and mix to incorporate.

Drop dough, ½ tablespoon at time, onto lightly greased baking sheet. Bake at 350 degrees 6 to 10 minutes or until golden brown. Makes about 3 ½ dozen.

Notes:

HILLARY'S CHOCOLATE CHIP-OATMEAL COOKIES

Readers thanked First Lady Hillary Rodham Clinton for sharing this now-famous chocolate chip oatmeal cookie.

1 ½ cups flour
1 teaspoon salt
1 teaspoon baking soda
1 cup shortening
1 cup brown sugar, packed
½ cup granulated sugar
1 teaspoon vanilla
2 eggs
2 cups oats
1 (12-ounce) package semisweet chocolate chips

Combine flour, salt and baking soda. Beat together shortening, sugars and vanilla in large bowl until creamy. Add eggs, beating until light and fluffy. Gradually beat in flour mixture and oats. Stir in chocolate chips.

Drop batter by well-rounded teaspoonfuls onto greased baking sheets. Bake at 350 degrees 8 to 10 minutes or until golden. Cool cookies on baking sheets on wire rack 2 minutes. Remove cookies to wire rack to cool completely. Makes about 5 dozen cookies.

JULIENNE'S BREAKFAST COOKIES

Julienne's cafe in Pasadena named these nutritious morsels "breakfast cookies" because they are almost a complete breakfast-in-a-cookie.

3 cups rolled oats
2 cups flour
1 cup whole wheat flour
2 cups dark brown sugar, lightly packed
2 teaspoons ground nutmeg
1 ½ teaspoons salt
1 ½ teaspoons baking soda
1 cup butter, softened
1 cup buttermilk
2 cups assorted diced dried fruit and raisins
1 ½ cups walnuts

Combine oats, flour, whole wheat flour, brown sugar, nutmeg, salt and baking soda. With pastry blender or fork, cut in softened butter until mixture is moist and crumbly. Sir in buttermilk. Add dried fruits and walnuts. Drop by tablespoonful onto baking sheet and bake at 375 degrees until browned, about 12 minutes. Makes about 4 dozen cookies.

❖

MRS. JOST'S PERSIMMON COOKIES

Here's a cherished recipe for persimmon cookies from a reader.

1 cup sugar
½ cup butter
1 egg
2 cups flour
1 teaspoon ground nutmeg
½ teaspoon ground cinnamon
½ teaspoon ground cloves
1 cup chopped walnuts
½ cup raisins, optional
1 cup pureed persimmon pulp
1 teaspoon baking soda

Cream sugar and butter together. Beat in egg.

In bowl sift flour, nutmeg, cinnamon and cloves together. Stir in nuts and raisins.

Puree persimmon pulp until smooth and stir in baking soda. Add persimmon mixture and dry ingredients alternately to creamed butter and sugar mixture, mixing well after each addition.

Drop batter by heaping teaspoons on greased baking sheet. Bake at 350 degrees 15 minutes. Makes about 2 dozen cookies.

SCRIPPS' CHOCOLATE CHIP-OATMEAL COOKIES

A reader who stayed at the Scripps Clinic in La Jolla first requested these chewy cookies.

¾ cup margarine
1 cup brown sugar, packed
¼ cup granulated sugar
1 egg
¼ cup water
1 teaspoon vanilla
2 ½ cups oats
¾ cup plus 2 tablespoons flour
½ teaspoon salt
½ teaspoon baking soda
½ cup chocolate pieces

Beat together margarine, sugars, egg, water and vanilla until creamy. Combine oats, flour, salt, baking soda and chocolate pieces. Mix well. Place about ¼ cup dough per cookie on greased baking sheet and bake at 350 degrees 12 to 15 minutes. Makes 1½ dozen.

MOLASSES COOKIES

A reader, who won a Times "My Best Recipe" prize for the recipe in 1965, sent us her version of the a chewy molasses cookie often requested by readers.

1 cup shortening
1 cup sugar
1 cup molasses
4 cups flour
2 teaspoons soda
1 teaspoon ginger
$\frac{1}{2}$ teaspoon cloves or cinnamon
$\frac{1}{2}$ teaspoon salt
1 cup warm water

Cream shortening and sugar. Blend in molasses. Sift together flour, soda, ginger, cloves and salt. Add to creamed mixture alternately with warm water. Drop by teaspoonfuls, 2 inches apart, onto greased cookie sheet. Bake at 375 degrees 8 to 10 minutes. Don't overbake and cookies will be moist and soft. Makes about 8 dozen cookies.

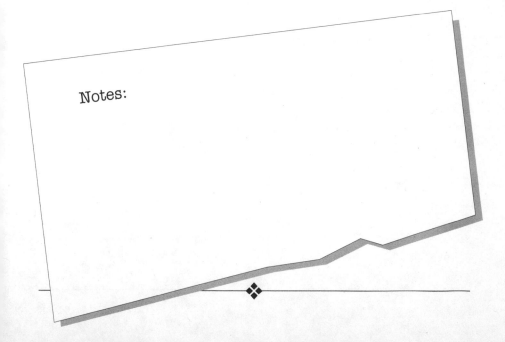

Notes:

LIKE WILL WRIGHT'S MACAROONS

These macaroons are reminiscent of those served at such ice cream parlors as Will Wright's in Westwood, California, during the first half of the century.

1 (7-ounce) tube almond paste
¾ cup sugar
2 egg whites, lightly beaten
1 tablespoon flour

Combine almond paste and sugar. Add lightly beaten egg whites until mixture is smooth and not runny. Mix in flour until well mixed.

Drop by teaspoonful (or less for smaller cookies) onto greased and floured foil-lined baking sheet. Bake at 325 degrees 15 minutes (10 to 12 minutes for smaller cookies). Cool slightly before removing. Makes 2 dozen cookies.

NO BAKE

BOURBON BALLS

These easy, no-bake cookies are frequently requested during the holidays.

> *1 cup finely crushed vanilla wafers*
> *Powdered sugar*
> *1 to 1 1/2 cups finely chopped pecans*
> *2 tablespoons unsweetened cocoa powder*
> *2 tablespoons light corn syrup*
> *1/4 cup bourbon, dark rum or brandy*
> *1/4 cup granulated or powdered sugar*

Combine crushed wafers, 1 cup powdered sugar, pecans and cocoa powder. Add corn syrup and bourbon and mix well. With dampened hands, shape into 1-inch balls. Roll in granulated or powdered sugar.

Pack loosely in tin, separating layers with wax paper. Cover tightly and store at least 24 hours for best flavor. Makes about 4 dozen.

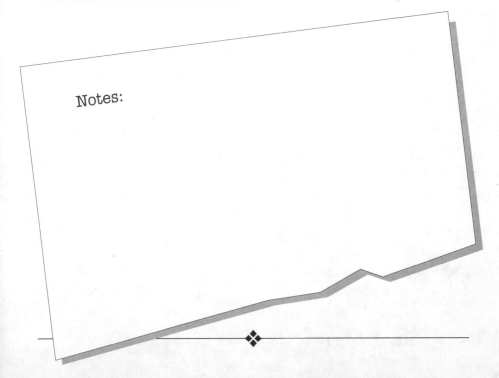

Notes:

MUD BALLS

Mud Balls make an excellent treat for children too.

> *3 cups quick-cooking oats*
> *3 tablespoons unsweetened cocoa powder*
> *½ cup dry milk*
> *½ teaspoon salt*
> *1 cup raisins*
> *½ cup chunky peanut butter*
> *½ cup honey*
> *2 teaspoons vanilla*

Combine oats, cocoa powder, dry milk and salt in large bowl and mix well.

Fold in raisins, peanut butter, honey and vanilla and mix well. Mixture will be sticky, so use 1 hand to mix thoroughly. Form tablespoonfuls of dough into balls. Place balls on platter and serve. Store in refrigerator in covered container. Makes about 7 dozen.

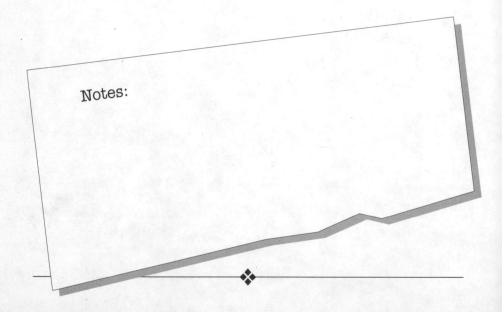

Notes:

❖

MIRACLES *(No-Bake Missouri Cookies)*

Those who request a no-bake cookie usually are asking for Miracles made with oats and nuts.

2 cups sugar
3 to 5 tablespoons cocoa powder
½ cup milk
½ cup butter
Dash salt
1 teaspoon vanilla
½ cup peanut butter, optional
½ cup coconut
3 cups quick-cooking oats
½ cup chopped nuts

Combine sugar, cocoa, milk, butter and salt in 2-quart saucepan. Cook and stir until butter melts and mixture comes to full rolling boil. Cook 1 to 2 minutes. Remove from heat. Stir in vanilla and peanut butter. Mix in coconut, oats and nuts. Mix well. Drop by teaspoonfuls onto wax paper. Cool until firm. Makes about 5 dozen.

SHAPED & ROLLED

CHINESE FORTUNE COOKIES

The trick to shaping these cookies is to keep the cookie warm while folding.

¾ cup butter or margarine, softened
2 cups sugar
1 teaspoon vanilla
3 eggs
1 cup sifted flour
5 dozen paper fortunes

Cream together butter and sugar until fluffy. Blend in vanilla. Add eggs, 1 at time, beating well after each addition. Beat in flour. Drop 6 rounded teaspoons dough at least 2 inches apart on greased and floured baking sheets. Bake at 375 degrees 15 to 20 minutes, or until edges are well browned.

Remove from oven. Loosen cookies carefully with wide spatula, keeping pan warm. Gently fold each cookie in half, wrapping paper fortunes inside and keeping top of cookies on outside. Pinch points together. Cool. Makes 5 dozen.

Notes:

FLORENTINES

These lacy cookies are wonderful on a tea table.

⅓ cup sifted flour
Dash salt
¼ teaspoon baking soda
¼ cup butter or margarine
⅓ cup brown sugar, packed
2 tablespoons light corn syrup
1 egg, well beaten
½ teaspoon vanilla
½ cup flake coconut
2 squares semisweet chocolate

Sift together flour, salt and baking soda. Cream butter and add brown sugar gradually, beating until light and fluffy. Add corn syrup and egg and beat well.

Stir in flour mixture, vanilla and coconut. Drop by teaspoons on greased baking sheet about 2 inches apart. Spread into thin rounds. Bake at 350 degrees about 10 minutes. Remove at once from baking sheet.

Heat chocolate over hot water until partly melted. Remove from hot water and stir rapidly until entirely melted. Drizzle chocolate in lacy pattern over cookie or halfway dip cookie into chocolate, then place on wax paper to harden. Makes 1 dozen.

❖

WORLD'S BEST SUGAR COOKIES *(Mother's Sugar Cookies)*

Scores of readers mailed us their recipes for these outstanding cookies, which we once lost.

1 cup butter
1 cup powdered sugar
Granulated sugar
2 eggs
1 cup oil
2 teaspoons vanilla
1 teaspoon baking soda
1 teaspoon cream of tartar
½ teaspoon salt
5 cups flour

In medium bowl cream butter with powdered sugar and 1 cup granulated sugar. Beat in eggs until smooth. Slowly stir in oil, vanilla, baking soda, cream of tartar, salt and flour.

Chill for easy handling. Shape into walnut-size balls. Dip in sugar. Place on baking sheet and press down. Bake at 350 degrees 10 to 12 minutes. Makes about 4 dozen cookies.

MARTIN LUTHER KING HOSPITAL OATMEAL COOKIES

When readers requested oatmeal cookies made with rolled oats from Martin Luther King Hospital, we all were pleasantly surprised with the results.

1 ½ cups raisins
Water
2 eggs
1 ½ teaspoons vanilla
1 cup shortening
¾ cup plus 2 tablespoons sugar
1 ⅓ cups brown sugar, packed
2 cups flour
1 ⅛ teaspoons salt
½ teaspoon baking soda
2 ⅛ teaspoons baking powder
3 ¾ cups oats

Place raisins in bowl and add enough warm water to cover. Soak 10 minutes. Drain thoroughly and set aside.

Combine eggs, 2 tablespoons water, vanilla, shortening and sugars in mixer bowl. Sift together flour, salt, baking soda and baking powder. Add to egg mixture and beat at low speed 2 to 3 minutes or until smooth. Add oats and raisins and mix until blended. Mold into 2-inch-thick rolls. Wrap in wax paper and chill. Slice rolls into ½-inch slices and place on baking sheets. Flatten to ¼-inch thickness and bake at 375 degrees 10 to 12 minutes. Makes about 32 large cookies.

PIES

O f all recipes requested, the pie, as well as cake, categories top the list, which means that there are a disproportionately greater number of these recipes than most other desserts. Among the several dozen pie recipes, you are bound to discover a favorite or two. Perhaps it will be *Key Lime Pie, Green Tomato Pie, Cherry Pie* or *Grasshopper Pie*. Whatever the favorite, all of these pie recipes have passed the test of time. Be sure to check page 256 for information about using raw eggs and egg substitutes.

Dear S.O.S.:
     We couldn't get over the taste of the Pecan Tart at Spago's restaurant in Hollywood. Will Wolfgang Puck part with the recipe?
     —Cheryl

Dear Cheryl:
     Puck was delighted to share the recipe, and many readers will thank you for asking.

APPLE

CRUSTLESS APPLE PIE

Here's a pie that is classified as truly "low-calorie" because it is made without a crust, uses artificial sweetener and has a topping made with dry nonfat milk instead of whipping cream.

2 medium apples, peeled, cored and sliced
1 envelope unflavored gelatin
¾ cup water
Liquid sweetener equal to ⅓ cup sugar
¼ teaspoon ground cinnamon
⅛ teaspoon ground nutmeg
2 tablespoons lemon juice
Homemade Whipped Topping (Page 249)

Place apples in 8-inch pie pan. Soften gelatin in water and heat until dissolved. Stir in sweetener, cinnamon, nutmeg and lemon juice. Pour over apples. Bake at 325 degrees 1 hour or until apples are tender. Cool and chill. Serve with Whipped Topping. Makes 1 (8-inch) pie.

RUTH'S CHRIS STEAK HOUSE DUTCH APPLE PIE

Ruth's Chris Steak House produces this fabulous Dutch apple pie with streusel crumb topping probably originating with the Pennsylvania Dutch.

1¾ cups water
6 tablespoons granulated sugar
2 tablespoons brown sugar, packed
Dash nutmeg
¼ teaspoon ground cinnamon
¼ ounce orange liqueur
4 medium apples, peeled, cored and sliced into wheels
3 tablespoons raisins
2½ tablespoons cornstarch
1 partially baked (9- or 10-inch) pie shell
Crumb Topping

Combine 1½ cups water, sugars, nutmeg, cinnamon and liqueur in large saucepan. Bring almost to boil. Add apple slices and cook 4 minutes. Add raisins. Cook 2 minutes or until apples are no longer crisp, but not mushy.

Mix cornstarch into ¼ cup water and add to apple mixture. Continue cooking, stirring until slightly thickened and clear. Pour into partially baked pie shell, making slight mound. Crumble topping on pie, making large mound, being sure to cover filling completely. Bake at 350 degrees 45 to 50 minutes, or until browned. Makes 1 (9- or 10-inch) pie.

CRUMB TOPPING

½ cup brown sugar, packed
½ cup granulated sugar
1 ¾ cups self-rising flour, lightly packed
¾ teaspoon ground nutmeg
½ teaspoon ground cinnamon
¼ teaspoon vanilla
½ cup plus 2 tablespoons butter, softened

Combine sugars, flour, nutmeg and cinnamon, mixing thoroughly. In another bowl, combine vanilla and butter, then add to dry mixture. Be sure butter is mixed in thoroughly. Consistency should be moist but not wet, and dry but not powdery. Makes 4 cups streusel.

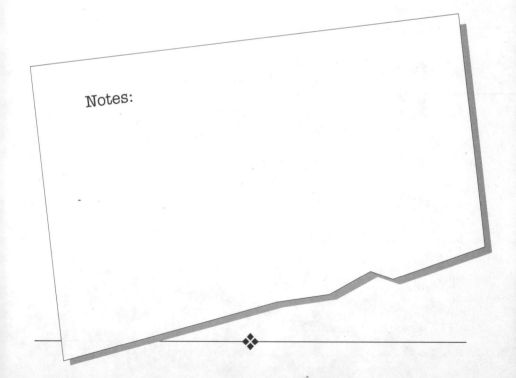

Notes:

SODA CRACKER PIE *(Mock Apple Pie)*

Here's the classic Depression-era pie that is also known as Mock Apple Pie. It tastes like apple pie but isn't.

2 eggs
1 cup sugar
1 teaspoon baking powder
1 cup chopped walnuts
1 cup crushed soda crackers
1 teaspoon vanilla

Beat eggs and combine with sugar and baking powder. Add nuts and soda crackers and stir in vanilla. Pour into greased 8- or 9-inch pie plate and bake at 325 degrees 30 minutes. Makes 6 servings.

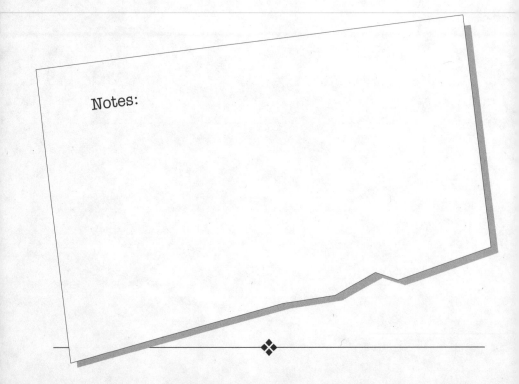

Notes:

CHOCOLATE

Brown Derby's Black Bottom Pie

This recipe was shared by the famous Brown Derby in Hollywood and is one of our favorites.

1 envelope unflavored gelatin
2 tablespoons cold water
½ cup milk
2 tablespoons sugar
Dash salt
1 teaspoon vanilla
1 egg yolk
3 ounces sweet or semisweet chocolate
2 cups whipping cream
1 (9-inch) baked pie shell

Soften gelatin in cold water. Bring milk to boil in top of double boiler. Beat together sugar, salt, ½ teaspoon vanilla and egg yolk until light and creamy. Add small amount of milk to egg mixture, blending well. Return to remaining milk in pan. Cook, stirring, over hot water until mixture barely comes to boil. Remove from heat and stir in gelatin until dissolved.

Grate 2 ounces chocolate. Add to custard and stir over hot water until chocolate is melted. Remove from heat and beat with rotary beater until custard is smooth.

Chill until custard reaches cream-like consistency. Whip 1 cup cream until stiff and fold into custard with remaining ½ teaspoon vanilla. Turn into baked pie shell and chill until firm.

At serving time, whip remaining 1 cup cream until stiff and spread over filling. Shave remaining 1 ounce chocolate and sprinkle over top of pie. Makes 1 (9-inch) pie.

CHOCOLATE CHIFFON PIE

Many readers request recipes for a standard Chocolate Chiffon Pie.

1 envelope unflavored gelatin
½ cup sugar
⅓ cup cocoa powder
Water
1 tablespoon lemon juice
½ cup instant nonfat dry milk
1 (9-inch) baked pie shell

Combine gelatin and sugar in small saucepan. Stir in cocoa and 1 cup water. Cook over low heat, stirring constantly, until gelatin and sugar are dissolved and mixture is smooth, about 5 minutes. Set aside to cool.

In small electric mixer bowl, combine ½ cup cold water, lemon juice and nonfat dry milk. Beat at high speed until stiff, about 6 minutes. Pour dissolved gelatin mixture into deep mixing bowl over ice water. Stir until mixture is cooled and syrupy.

Remove bowl from ice water and beat mixture until very foamy. Fold whipped nonfat milk mixture into gelatin. Turn into pie shell. Chill until set, about 3 hours. Garnish with additional whipped nonfat dry milk and chocolate curls, if desired. Makes 1 (9-inch) pie.

❖

German's Sweet Chocolate Pie

This pie was a variation on the Baker's German's Sweet Chocolate Cake that became popular when the recipe appeared on the chocolate wrapper.

1 (4-ounce) package sweet chocolate
1/4 cup butter or margarine
1 (13-ounce) can evaporated milk
1 1/2 cups sugar
1/8 teaspoon salt
3 tablespoons cornstarch
2 eggs
1 teaspoon vanilla
1 unbaked (9- or 10-inch) pie shell
1/3 cup flaked coconut
1/2 cup chopped pecans

Melt chocolate with butter over low heat. Gradually blend in milk. Thoroughly mix sugar, salt and cornstarch. Beat in eggs and vanilla. Gradually blend in chocolate mixture. Pour into pie shell.

Combine coconut and pecans and sprinkle over filling. Bake at 375 degrees 45 to 50 minutes or until puffed. Filling will be soft, but will set while cooling. Chill at least 4 hours before cutting. Makes 1 (9- or 10-inch) pie.

Note: If top browns too quickly, cover loosely with foil during last 15 minutes.

JUSTICE LILLIE'S CHOCOLATE MOUSSE PIE

Justice Mildred Lillie of the Court of Appeals in Los Angeles was also a creative cook who developed this recipe according to the popular chocolate mousses served in restaurants during the '70s.

8 eggs, separated
1 ½ cups plus 3 tablespoons sugar
2 teaspoons vanilla
¼ teaspoon salt
½ cup brandy
10 ounces unsweetened chocolate
2 ounces semisweet chocolate
¾ cup butter, softened
½ cup coffee
½ cups whipping cream
Chocolate Crust
Cherry Cordials

Combine egg yolks, 1½ cups sugar, vanilla, salt and brandy in top of double boiler. Place over simmering water and beat until pale yellow and thick, about 8 to 10 minutes. Remove from water and set aside.

Melt both unsweetened and semisweet chocolate in top of double boiler over hot water. When melted, remove from water and beat in butter, bit at time.

Gradually beat chocolate into egg yolk mixture until smooth. Chocolate mixture will congeal and become very stiff. Beat in coffee.

Beat egg whites (at room temperature) into soft peaks. Gradually beat in remaining 3 tablespoons sugar until stiff peaks form. Beat 1 cup beaten egg whites into chocolate mixture to thin, then carefully fold in remaining beaten egg whites until thoroughly incorporated.

Beat whipping cream until stiff and gently fold into chocolate mixture. Pour into prepared Chocolate Crust and chill overnight in refrigerator. Garnish with Cherry Cordials. Makes 1 (9-inch) pie.

Note: See warning on the use of raw eggs, page 256.

CHOCOLATE CRUST

⅔ (8½-ounce) package dark chocolate wafers
2 tablespoons butter, melted

Grind wafers in blender container until crumbs are very fine. Combine butter with crumbs and pat onto sides and bottom of buttered 9-inch springform pan. Bake at 325 degrees 10 minutes. Remove from oven and cool completely.

CHERRY CORDIALS

13 maraschino cherries with stems, drained
½ cup brandy
5 ounces semisweet chocolate

Soak cherries in brandy and place in freezer. Melt chocolate over hot water. When cherries are frozen, dry on paper towels. Then quickly dip cherries, 1 at time, into chocolate, swirling around by stem until completely covered. Chocolate will harden almost immediately. Place on wax-paper-lined rack in refrigerator until ready to use.

❖

MILK CHOCOLATE BAR PIE

Candy-bar pies had a long run between the '50s and '80s.

> *Chocolate Petal Crust*
> *1 (¹/₂-pound) milk chocolate bar or milk chocolate bar with almonds*
> *¹/₃ cup milk*
> *1 ¹/₂ cups miniature or 15 regular marshmallows*
> *1 cup whipping cream*
> *Whipped cream topping or chilled cherry pie filling, optional*

Prepare Chocolate Petal Crust and set aside. Break chocolate bar, chopping almonds, if used, into small pieces. Melt with milk in top of double boiler over hot water. Add marshmallows, stirring until melted. Cool completely.

Whip cream until stiff, then fold into chocolate mixture. Pour into Chocolate Petal Crust. Chill several hours until firm. Garnish with whipped cream topping or pie filling. Makes 1 (9-inch) pie.

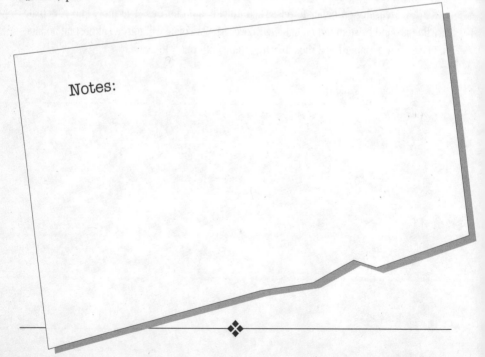

Notes:

CHOCOLATE PETAL CRUST

½ cup butter or margarine
1 cup sugar
1 egg
1 teaspoon vanilla
1 ¼ cups flour
½ cup cocoa powder
¾ teaspoon baking soda
¼ teaspoon salt

Cream butter, sugar, egg and vanilla until light and fluffy. Combine flour, cocoa, baking soda and salt. Add to creamed mixture. Shape soft dough into 2 (1½-inch) rolls. Wrap in wax paper. Chill until firm.

Cut 1 roll into ⅛-inch slices. Arrange, edges touching, on bottom and sides of greased 9-inch pie pan. (Small spaces in crust will not affect pie.) Bake at 375 degrees 8 to 10 minutes. Cool.

Note: Freeze any leftover dough for use for pie crust or cookies.

BUTTERSCOTCH DREAM PIE

It took pie chef Bev Schneckle, who once cooked for family and hired hands on a ranch, "some experimenting to make a publishable recipe" for the reader who requested the pie recipe.

1 (8-ounce) package cream cheese, at room temperature
1 cup powdered sugar
2 ½ cups whipped topping
⅓ cup pecan pieces
1 (10-inch) baked pie shell, cooled to room temperature
⅓ cup brown sugar, packed
3 cups cold milk
2 (3.4-ounce) packages instant butterscotch pudding mix
2 tablespoons butterscotch schnapps, optional
1 teaspoon butter, melted
Whipped topping
Chopped pecans

Beat cream cheese with powdered sugar until smooth. Mix in whipped topping. Sprinkle pecan pieces on cooled, baked pie shell. Spread cream cheese mixture in pie shell.

Mix brown sugar and cold milk until dissolved. Add pudding mix, stirring with wire whip until smooth and starting to thicken. Mix according to package directions. Add butterscotch schnapps and butter. Mix well.

Allow to stand up to 5 minutes or until almost but not completely set, with whip indentations remaining somewhat visible. Carefully pour on top of cream cheese mixture, spreading evenly. Chill until set.

Spread ¼ to ½ inch whipped topping on top of pudding. Or pipe whipped topping from pastry tube in dollops or around edge of pie. Garnish with sprinkling of chopped pecans. Makes 1 (10-inch) pie.

❖

KAHLUA PIE

This chiffon-type liqueur pie became famous during the '60s when liqueur companies began campaigns for using liqueur in foods.

4 1/2 teaspoons unflavored gelatin
3/4 cup Kahlua
Sugar
4 egg yolks
4 egg whites
1/4 teaspoon salt
1 1/4 cups heavy whipping cream
1 (9-inch) pie shell, baked
Shaved unsweetened chocolate

In top of double-boiler off heat, soften gelatin with Kahlua until dissolved. Add 1/4 cup sugar and egg yolks and set in bottom of double boiler over hot, but not boiling, water. Warm, stirring constantly, until thickened. Cool.

Beat egg whites in large bowl until frothy. Add salt and beat until soft peaks form. Gradually beat in 1/4 cup sugar. Whip 1 cup whipping cream in separate bowl until stiff. Place on top of egg whites. Add cooled Kahlua mixture and gently fold together.

Refrigerate until mixture holds definite mound shape when dropped from spoon. Pile into pie shell and refrigerate 30 minutes before serving. Beat remaining 1/4 cup whipping cream until stiff. Spoon over pie and sprinkle with shaved chocolate. Makes 1 (9-inch) pie.

Note: See warning on the use of raw eggs, page 256.

HARRIS RANCH BANANA SPLIT PIE

Readers say that the Banana Split Pie at the Harris Ranch in Coalinga, Calif., is the best pie of its kind.

1 1/2 cups whipping cream
1 cup semisweet chocolate chips
Vanilla Custard
1 (9-inch) baked pie shell
1 large ripe banana, sliced
1 (8-ounce) can pineapple chunks, sliced in halves and well drained
1 (1/2-inch) thick, (8-inch) round white cake layer
3 ounces almonds, diced and toasted
Whole strawberries, about 10

Combine 1/2 cup whipping cream and chocolate chips in small saucepan. Gently heat over low heat until chocolate melts, stirring occasionally. Set aside to cool completely.

Pour 1 cup Vanilla Custard into pie shell. Arrange banana slices in layer over custard. Spread 1/2 cup Vanilla Custard on bananas. Arrange pineapple over custard. Spread on remaining 1/2 cup custard. Gently place cake layer on custard. Spread cooled chocolate mixture over cake slices.

Top with diced almonds. Whip remaining whipping cream. Fill pastry bag with whipped cream and pipe rosettes around and on center of pie. Garnish each rosette with whole strawberry. Makes 1 (9-inch) pie.

❖

VANILLA CUSTARD

2 eggs
2 tablespoons cornstarch
¼ cup sugar
⅛ teaspoon salt
1 ½ cups milk, scalded
1 teaspoon vanilla

Whisk eggs in top of double boiler. Whisk in cornstarch, sugar and salt until blended. Slowly stir hot milk into egg mixture. Place over simmering water that does not touch top pan and cook, stirring constantly, until custard coats metal spoon. Immediately remove from heat. Cool immediately by pouring custard into cold bowl or by setting pan in bowl of ice water. Stir in vanilla. Cover and chill. Makes 2 cups.

LULU BELLE'S GRASSHOPPER PIE

A reader requested a grasshopper pie recipe containing marshmallows and got it.

²/₃ cup milk
24 marshmallows
2 ounces green creme de menthe
1 ounce white creme de cacao
1 cup whipping cream
Chocolate Crust
Whipped cream

Scald milk in top of double boiler over simmering water and add marshmallows. Cook and stir over simmering water until marshmallows are melted. Cool to room temperature. Add creme de menthe and creme de cacao.

Whip cream and fold into marshmallow mixture. Turn into Chocolate Crust and freeze. Serve with whipped cream, if desired. Makes 1 (9-inch) pie.

CHOCOLATE CRUST

1 ¼ cups crushed chocolate cookie wafers
⅓ cup melted butter

Mix chocolate wafers with melted butter. Pat into 9-inch pie pan and chill.

❖

Macadamia Nut Cream Pie

A Hawaiian Macadamia Nut Cream Pie from the Kaanapali Beach Hotel is a top favorite in the islands.

1 ⅓ cups milk
¾ cup sugar
Chopped toasted macadamia nuts
Dash salt
1 teaspoon vanilla
3 eggs, separated
1 tablespoon cornstarch
1 baked (8-inch) pastry shell
Whipped cream

Combine 1 cup milk, ¼ cup sugar, ¼ cup nuts, salt and vanilla in top of double boiler. Place over boiling water and scald. Combine remaining ⅓ cup milk, egg yolks and cornstarch and add to hot milk mixture.

Cook, stirring, until thickened. Remove from heat and cool slightly. Beat egg whites with remaining ½ cup sugar until stiff. Carefully fold into milk mixture and turn into pastry shell. When cool, top with whipped cream and sprinkle with additional chopped nuts, if desired. Makes 1 (8-inch) pie.

Note: See warning on the use of raw eggs, page 256.

SYCAMORE INN CHEESE PIE

A pure and simple cheese pie with a fabulous sour cream topping in the true California cheese pie tradition.

1 1/2 (8-ounce) packages cream cheese, at room temperature
3 large eggs
1/2 cup sugar
Juice of 1/2 lemon
1 teaspoon vanilla
Graham Cracker Crust
Sour Cream Topping

In electric mixer bowl, using wire whip, mix cream cheese, eggs, sugar, lemon juice and vanilla. Spread into Graham Cracker Crust. Bake at 350 degrees 35 minutes. Cool completely. Spread Sour Cream Topping over cooled, baked filling. Refrigerate to cool and set. Makes 1 (9-inch) pie.

GRAHAM CRACKER CRUST

1 1/4 cups graham cracker crumbs
1 tablespoon plus 1 teaspoon flour
1/4 cup clarified butter

Mix crumbs and flour in metal pan or skillet. Heat over very low heat or at 350 degrees 5 minutes or until warmed. Add butter until well mixed. Pat crumbs onto bottom and sides of 9-inch pie plate until crumbs form solid crust.

❖

SOUR CREAM TOPPING
½ cup sugar
2 teaspoons vanilla
4 cups sour cream

By hand or with wire whisk, beat together sugar, vanilla and sour cream until well blended.

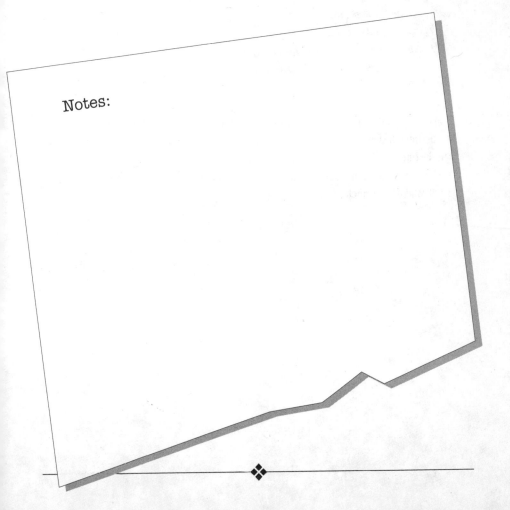

Notes:

FRUIT

Piña Colada Pie

When Piña Colada became a fad drink, cakes and pies like this one soon followed course.

2 envelopes unflavored gelatin
½ cup sugar
¼ teaspoon salt
1 (20-ounce) can crushed pineapple
1 ½ cups buttermilk
¼ cup lemon juice
½ teaspoon almond extract
½ cup flaked coconut
1 cup frozen nondairy whipped topping, thawed
1 (9-inch) graham cracker pie shell

Combine gelatin, sugar and salt in medium saucepan. Blend in pineapple with liquid. Heat, stirring constantly, until gelatin is dissolved. Remove from heat.

Stir in buttermilk, lemon juice and almond extract. Chill until thickened but not set. Beat with mixer until fluffy. Fold in coconut and nondairy topping. Chill until set. Pour into pie shell. Makes 1 (9-inch) pie.

❖

Clifton's Fruit-Nut Torte

Clifton's Fruit-Nut Torte is served in their cafeterias in Los Angeles.

1 egg
¾ cup granulated sugar
1 cup fruit cocktail, undrained
1 cup flour
1 teaspoon baking soda
¼ teaspoon salt
½ cup walnuts, chopped
¼ cup brown sugar
Hot Icing
Whipped cream, optional

Beat egg, granulated sugar and fruit cocktail. Stir in flour, baking soda and salt and mix thoroughly. Pour into greased 9-inch round cake pan. Combine walnuts and brown sugar. Sprinkle evenly over top of batter.

Bake at 350 degrees 30 minutes. Pour Hot Icing over cake as it comes out of oven. Serve with whipped cream, if desired. Makes 1 (9-inch) pie.

HOT ICING

¾ cup sugar
½ cup evaporated milk
⅓ cup butter or margarine
½ teaspoon vanilla

Combine sugar, evaporated milk and butter in saucepan. Bring to boil. Boil 3 minutes, stirring. Remove from heat. Add vanilla.

❖

ZWIEBACK PUDDING PIE

This old-fashioned zwieback-crust pie topped with meringue is just the ticket on a wintry day.

1 cup ground zwieback or biscotti crumbs
¼ cup plus 2 tablespoons sugar
1 tablespoon cinnamon
¼ cup melted butter
1 egg yolk
Custard Filling
Meringue Topping

Mix crumbs, sugar and cinnamon. Reserve 1 tablespoon mixture for topping. Thoroughly blend butter and egg yolk into remaining crumb mixture and press into 9-inch pie plate. Bake at 350 degrees 15 minutes. Cool on wire rack.

Pour Custard Filling into cooled pie shell. Cover with Meringue Topping and sprinkle with reserved crumb mixture. Bake at 400 degrees 8 to 10 minutes, until set and slightly golden. Makes 1 (9-inch) pie.

CUSTARD FILLING

⅔ cup sugar
2 tablespoons cornstarch
2 cups milk
2 egg yolks, beaten
1 teaspoon vanilla

Stir together sugar and cornstarch. Stir in milk until blended. Heat milk mixture and carefully stir in egg yolks. Cook and stir over low heat until thickened. Remove from heat and stir in vanilla. Cool slightly. Makes 2 cups.

❖

MERINGUE TOPPING

2 egg whites
¼ cup sugar
Dash salt

Beat egg whites until frothy. Gradually stir in sugar and salt and beat until stiff peaks form.

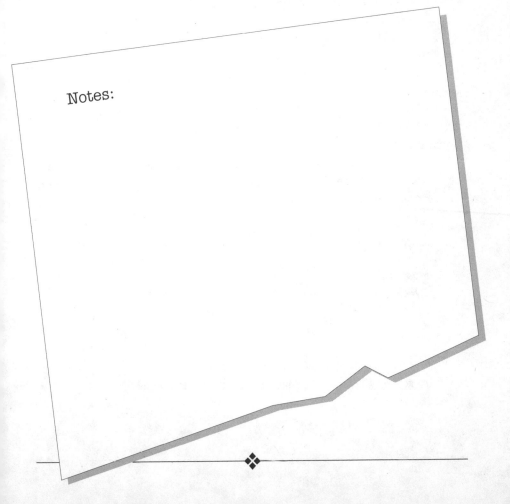

Notes:

WILLOW'S COCONUT CREAM PIE

A great coconut cream pie from Hawaii.

2 cups milk
½ cup sugar
Dash salt
Grated fresh coconut
4 egg yolks
3 tablespoons cornstarch
1 tablespoon butter or margarine
1 teaspoon vanilla
1 (9-inch) baked pie shell
Meringue

Combine milk, sugar, salt and ¼ cup grated coconut in medium saucepan. Cook until mixture is very hot. Beat egg yolks, then blend in cornstarch and little water. Add egg yolk mixture to milk mixture. Cook and stir about 1 minute. Add butter and vanilla.

Cool filling and pour into pie shell. Swirl meringue onto pie, making sure it is sealed to edge of pie shell. Sprinkle with grated coconut. Bake at 400 degrees until golden brown. Cool completely. Makes 1 (9-inch) pie.

MERINGUE

4 to 6 egg whites
¼ teaspoon cream of tartar
Sugar

Beat egg whites with cream of tartar until soft peaks form. Gradually add 1 tablespoon sugar for each egg white used. Continue beating until stiff peaks form.

CRANBERRY-PECAN PIE

Fresh or frozen, cranberries are a good berry to keep in mind for pies the year-round.

1 cup flour
¼ cup cornmeal
¼ teaspoon salt
⅓ cup shortening
¼ cup cold water
4 eggs
½ cup brown sugar, packed
¾ cup light corn syrup
¼ cup pancake syrup
¼ cup butter or margarine, melted
1 teaspoon vanilla
1 cup chopped pecans
¾ cup chopped fresh or frozen cranberries, thawed
Whipped cream or ice cream, optional

Combine flour, cornmeal and salt in medium bowl. Cut in shortening until mixture resembles coarse meal. Add water, 1 tablespoon at a time, stirring lightly until mixture forms ball.

Wrap dough securely and chill about 30 minutes. Roll dough on lightly floured surface to form 13-inch circle. Fit loosely into 9-inch pie plate. Turn edges under and flute. Bake at 425 degrees 7 minutes. Cool.

In medium bowl, beat together eggs and brown sugar. Slowly add corn and pancake syrups, butter and vanilla, mixing well. Stir in pecans and cranberries.

Pour into partially baked pie crust. Bake at 325 degrees 40 to 45 minutes or until set. Cool thoroughly. Serve with whipped cream or ice cream, if desired. Makes 1 (9-inch) pie.

DOUBLE-CRUST PINEAPPLE PIE

Transplanted New Yorkers often request a Double-Crust Pineapple Pie commonly found in supermarkets on the East Coast.

> *Pastry for 2-crust pie*
> *1 cup sugar*
> *¼ teaspoon salt*
> *3 tablespoons cornstarch*
> *1 (1-pound 4-ounce) can crushed pineapple*
> *1 tablespoon lemon juice*

Divide dough in half, roll out and fit half into 9-inch pie plate. Combine sugar, salt and cornstarch in saucepan and blend well. Stir in pineapple with syrup and lemon juice. Cook over medium heat, stirring constantly until pineapple mixture thickens and comes to boil.

Pour pineapple mixture into pastry-lined pan and cover with top crust. Make slits in crust and bake at 425 degrees 25 to 30 minutes. Makes 1 (9-inch) pie.

NESSELRODE PIE

Readers who remember tasting this old-fashioned mixed candied fruit pie at seafood restaurants in New York can never forget it.

1 envelope unflavored gelatin
1 cup milk
¾ cup sugar
4 eggs, separated
¼ teaspoon salt
2 tablespoons rum
⅓ cup diced mixed candied fruit
1 (9-inch) baked pie shell
Shaved chocolate

Soften gelatin in milk in top of double boiler. Add ¼ cup sugar, egg yolks and salt. Beat just enough to blend. Cook, stirring, over simmering water until mixture thickens and coats metal spoon. Remove from heat and stir in rum. Chill until thickened, but not set.

Beat egg whites until foamy. Gradually add remaining ½ cup sugar, beating until stiff but not dry. Fold egg whites and fruit into gelatin mixture. Turn into pie shell and chill until firm. Garnish with chocolate shavings. Makes 1 (9-inch) pie.

Note: See warning on the use of raw eggs, page 256.

Old-Fashioned Raisin Pie

You can prepare this Old-Fashioned Raisin Pie with dark or golden raisins.

1 pound raisins
1 ½ cups boiling water
½ cup sugar
2 tablespoons flour
Shredded peel of 1 lemon
½ cup cold water
Pastry for 2-crust (9-inch) pie
1 tablespoon sugar
1 tablespoon milk

Place raisins in saucepan and cover with boiling water. Bring to boil, remove from heat and let raisins stand.

Meanwhile, combine sugar, flour and shredded peel. Stir in cold water to make smooth paste. Add to raisins and cook, stirring constantly, until thickened. Pour hot mixture into pastry-lined 9-inch pie plate. Cover with top crust and flute edges.

Mix sugar and milk. Brush top of pie with sugar mixture. Bake at 425 degrees 30 to 40 minutes. Makes 1 (9-inch) pie.

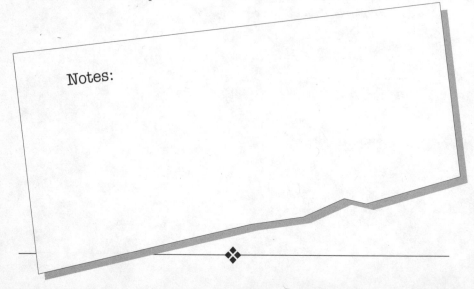

Notes:

PEACH PIE

Here's a basic double-crust peach pie recipe that is just as easy to make by substituting summer nectarines or plums for the peaches.

Pastry for 2-crust, 9-inch pie
6 cups peeled and sliced peaches,
   (about 2 pound), or half peaches and nectarines
1/2 cup sugar
3 tablespoons cornstarch
Dash salt
1/2 teaspoon nutmeg
1/2 cup sour cream
Milk
Sugar

Roll out half of pastry. Use to line bottom of 9-inch pie plate. Place peaches in pastry-lined pie plate or alternate layers of peaches and nectarines in pie plate. Combine sugar, cornstarch, salt, nutmeg and sour cream, mixing well. Pour over fruit. Roll out remaining pastry and make lattice top. Brush pastry with milk and sprinkle with sugar. Bake at 425 degrees for 10 minutes. Reduce heat to 350 degrees. Continue baking 45 to 50 minutes longer. Cool. Makes 1 (9-inch) pie.

SWEET CHERRY PIE

Serve it warm and top it with vanilla bean or other favorite flavor ice cream.

2 ¼ cups flour
1 ⅛ teaspoons salt
2 tablespoons ground almonds
⅔ cup plus 2 tablespoons shortening or ⅔ cup lard
4 to 5 tablespoons cold water
5 cups pitted sweet cherries
½ to ¾ cup sugar
1 tablespoon lemon juice
½ teaspoon almond extract
1 egg yolk

Combine 2 cups flour, 1 teaspoon salt and almonds in bowl. Cut in shortening. Sprinkle in water, 1 tablespoon at time, mixing until all flour is moistened and dough almost cleans sides of bowl. Gather dough into ball.

Divide dough in half and shape into 2 flattened rounds. Roll 1 portion to round 2 inches larger than inverted 9-inch pie plate. Fit pastry into pie plate leaving 1-inch overhang.

Toss cherries with sugar, lemon juice, remaining ¼ cup flour and ⅛ teaspoon salt and almond extract. Turn into pastry-lined pan. Roll out remaining dough and cut into ½-inch wide strips.

Place 5 to 7 strips across filling in pie plate. Weave 1 cross strip through center by folding back every other strip in opposite direction. Continue weaving until lattice is complete, folding back alternate strips each time cross-strip is added. Trim edges of strips. Fold trimmed edge of lower crust over ends of strips, building high edge. Seal and flute.

Bake at 425 degrees 25 minutes. Beat egg yolk and brush over lattice and crust edges. Continue to bake 15 minutes longer. If top crust browns too rapidly, cover with light tent or strips of foil. Serve warm or chilled. Makes 1 (9-inch) pie.

❖

LEMON

LEMON SPONGE PIE

A cake-like texture will appear on top with sauce on the bottom, similar to a cake-top pudding.

1 (8-inch) unbaked pie shell
1 tablespoon butter or margarine, softened
1 cup sugar
½ teaspoon salt
1 tablespoon flour
3 tablespoons lemon juice
1 teaspoon grated lemon peel
2 eggs, separated
1 cup milk

Bake pie shell at 425 degrees 10 minutes. Cool. Cream butter and sugar. Add salt, flour, lemon juice and peel. Beat egg yolks and add milk. Blend well with sugar mixture. Beat egg whites until stiff, then fold into filling. Pour filling into partially baked pie shell and bake at 350 degrees 35 minutes or until golden brown. (Cake-like mixture will be on top with sauce on bottom.) Makes 1 (8-inch) pie.

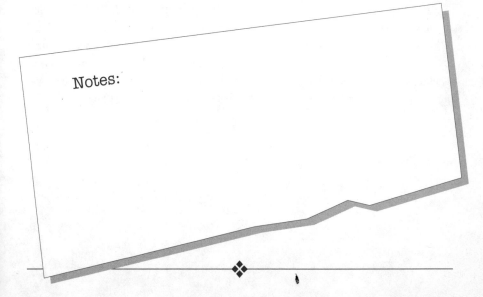

Notes:

FISH SHANTY'S BEAUTIFUL LEMON MERINGUE PIES

Our favorite lemon meringue pie recipe from the former Smith Bros. Fish Shanty.

3 cups water
2 ⅔ cups sugar
1 ½ teaspoons salt
1 tablespoon grated lemon peel
1 cup cold water
1 cup plus 2 tablespoons cornstarch
4 large or 5 small egg yolks
Juice of 4 lemons (¾ cup)
2 (9-inch) baked pie crusts
Meringue (Page 117)

Mix water, sugar, salt and lemon peel in top of double boiler. Bring to rolling boil over direct heat. Mix cold water and cornstarch in small bowl until completely dissolved. Add cornstarch mixture to bubbling sugar mixture, stirring constantly with wire whip until thoroughly blended and mixture starts to thicken and takes on clear appearance. Turn down heat if bubbles begin to pop while thickening.

Heat water in bottom of double boiler. Place sugar mixture in top of double boiler and continue to cook over boiling water about 10 minutes, stirring occasionally.

Turn off heat under double boiler. Beat yolks with lemon juice until blended. Stir into sugar mixture and blend thoroughly. Let stand 5 minutes, then pour into clean bowl. Cover and cool completely or overnight in refrigerator. Transfer to 2 baked pie crusts. Top with Meringue, forming peaks. Bake at 375 degrees 10 minutes until brown. Makes 2 (9-inch) pies.

❖

IMPOSSIBLE LEMON PIE

The distinguishing characteristic of all "impossible" pies is the self-made crust that forms during baking. This recipe for Impossible Lemon Pie is made in a blender.

1 cup milk
1 cup plus ½ teaspoon sugar
3/4 cup lemon juice
1 tablespoon grated lemon peel
½ cup buttermilk baking mix
4 eggs
¼ cup butter or margarine, diced
Whipped cream, optional

Place milk, 1 cup sugar, lemon juice, lemon peel, baking mix, eggs and butter in blender or food processor. Blend 2 to 3 minutes.

Pour batter into buttered 10-inch pie plate. Bake at 350 degrees 40 to 45 minutes or until center of pie is set. Sprinkle ½ teaspoon sugar over top of baked pie. Place under broiler until lightly browned. Cool and serve with whipped cream. Makes 1 (10-inch) pie.

SHAKER LEMON PIE

This tangy, sliced lemon pie recipe comes directly from the dining room at Shakertown, the restored Shaker village near Louisville, Kentucky.

> *2 large lemons*
> *2 cups sugar*
> *4 eggs, well beaten*
> *Pastry for 2-crust pie*

Slice lemons paper thin, including peel and removing seeds if desired. Combine with sugar and mix well. Let stand at least 2 hours or preferably overnight, mixing occasionally.

Fold in beaten eggs, mixing well. Arrange slices evenly in 9-inch pie shell. Cover with top crust. Cut several slits near center.

Bake at 450 degrees 15 minutes. Reduce heat and bake at 375 degrees 20 minutes longer or until knife inserted near center comes out clean. Cool before serving. Makes 1 (9-inch) pie.

Notes:

LIME

AVOCADO-LIME PIE

The recipe for no-sugar-added avocado-lime pie made with condensed milk is from the Glendale Adventist Hospital.

1 avocado
1 (14-ounce) can sweetened condensed milk
1 teaspoon grated lime zest
½ cup lime juice
2 egg yolks
Dash salt
1 (9-inch) baked pie shell
Mint leaves, optional

Peel avocado, remove pit and force pulp through sieve to make 1 cup. Combine condensed milk, lime zest and juice, lightly beaten egg yolks and salt. Stir until mixture thickens.

Fold in avocado, then turn into pastry shell. Chill several hours. Garnish with mint leaves. Makes 1 (9-inch) pie.

Note: See warning on the use of raw eggs, page 256.

❖

CANDLELIGHT KEY LIME PIE

The simplicity of this recipe containing only three major ingredients has helped maintain its popularity over the years.

Juice from 3 to 4 fresh key limes or small limes
2 (14-ounce) cans sweetened condensed milk
Green food color, optional
1 (9-inch) baked pie shell
Whipped cream, optional

Using hand whisk, slowly whip lime juice into milk until well mixed and thickened. Add food color. Turn into baked pie shell and chill in refrigerator 3 to 4 hours or overnight. Top with whipped cream. Makes 1 (9-inch) pie.

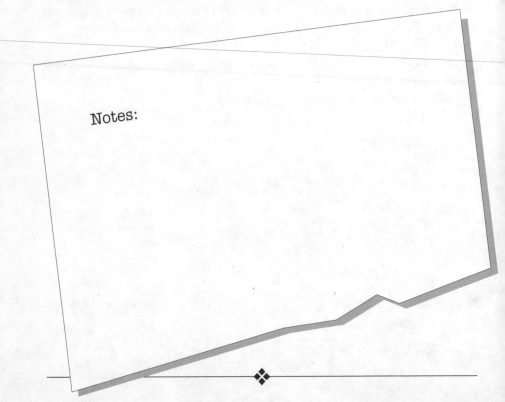

Notes:

PUMPKIN

PRALINE-PUMPKIN PIE

This recipe first appeared in old Los Angeles Times Home magazine in the '70s.

3 tablespoons butter
⅓ cup dark-brown sugar, packed
⅓ cup finely chopped pecans
1 (9-inch) pie crust
1 cup evaporated milk
½ cup water
2 eggs
1 (16-ounce) can pumpkin
½ cup granulated sugar
1 teaspoon ground cinnamon
¼ teaspoon ground cloves
¼ teaspoon ground nutmeg
1 teaspoon salt
½ cup whipping cream, whipped, optional
20 buttered pecan halves, optional

Cream butter with dark-brown sugar until fluffy. Stir in pecans and press mixture onto bottom of pie crust. Pierce bottom of crust with fork. Bake at 450 degrees 10 minutes. (This forms praline layer.) Cool.

Combine evaporated milk and water in saucepan and scald. Beat eggs in large bowl. Stir in pumpkin, granulated sugar, cinnamon, cloves, nutmeg and salt. Stir in hot milk mixture to blend. Spoon evenly over praline layer. Bake at 350 degrees 50 to 60 minutes until set, but still soft in center.

Cool and serve with whipped cream. Garnish with 20 buttered pecan halves. Makes 1 (9-inch) pie.

PUMPKIN-PERSIMMON PIE

Family coming for Thanksgiving? Serve them this unmistakably holiday dessert.

3 eggs, lightly beaten
1 cup canned pumpkin
²⁄₃ cup persimmon pulp (about 3 persimmons)
1 (14-ounce) can sweetened condensed milk
²⁄₃ cup sugar
¹⁄₄ teaspoon ground cloves
¹⁄₂ teaspoon ground ginger
1 teaspoon ground cinnamon
¹⁄₂ teaspoon salt
1 unbaked 9-inch pie shell
Whipped cream, optional

Combine eggs, pumpkin, persimmon pulp, condensed milk, sugar, cloves, ginger, cinnamon and salt. Mix well. Pour filling into pie shell. Bake at 350 degrees 45 minutes or until center is firm. Serve with whipped cream topping. Makes 1 (9-inch) pie.

❖

STRAWBERRY

Strawberry-Rhubarb Pie

Requests for Strawberry-Rhubarb Pie recipes appear mostly during the brief summer rhubarb season.

1 ½ cups sugar
3 tablespoons cornstarch
¼ teaspoon salt
1 pound rhubarb
1 box strawberries
Pastry for 2-crust (9- or 10-inch) pie
2 tablespoons butter or margarine

Combine sugar, cornstarch and salt and mix well. Cut rhubarb into ½-inch slices and wash, hull and slice berries. Add rhubarb and strawberries to sugar mixture and toss lightly to mix. Let stand while preparing pastry.

Roll out half of pastry and fit into 9- or 10-inch pie pan. Fill pie shell with fruit mixture. Dot with butter. Roll out remaining pastry and fit over pie. Seal and flute edges. Cut slits in top to allow steam to escape. Bake at 400 degrees 45 minutes or until syrup boils with heavy bubbles that do not burst. Serve warm with ice cream or whipped cream. Makes 1 (9- to 10-inch) pie.

VICKMAN'S STRAWBERRY PIE

Vickman's, once a thriving old-time cafeteria in downtown L.A.'s produce district, no longer exists but the glazed strawberry pie remains a reader favorite.

2 quarts strawberries
1/2 cup water
1 cup sugar
2 1/2 tablespoons cornstarch, potato starch or arrowroot
1 tablespoon butter or margarine
Few drops red food color, optional
1 baked 9-inch pie shell
Whipped cream

Wash, drain and hull strawberries. Place 2 cups of the strawberries in a bowl and crush. Mix the crushed strawberries with water, sugar and cornstarch. Simmer and stir about 2 minutes until thickened and clear. (It is important to cook cornstarch glaze until it loses its milk appearance to prevent cloudiness). Add butter and red food coloring. Put syrupy glaze through a fine strainer and cool 15 minutes. Pile remaining berries into baked pie shell. Carefully spoon glaze over the berries and serve topped with whipped cream. Makes 1 (9-inch) pie.

OTHER

CHESS PIE

An aficionado of chess pie shared his recipe with our magazine food editor back in 1980.

3 eggs
1 ½ cups sugar
1 tablespoon white cornmeal
1 tablespoon vinegar
½ cup butter, melted
1 teaspoon vanilla
1 (8-inch) unbaked pie shell

Beat eggs lightly in bowl. Stir in sugar, cornmeal and vinegar. Beat in melted butter and vanilla. Pour into pie shell and bake at 400 degrees 10 minutes. Reduce heat to 325 degrees and bake 45 to 55 minutes until golden and knife comes out clean when inserted near center. Makes 6 to 8 servings.

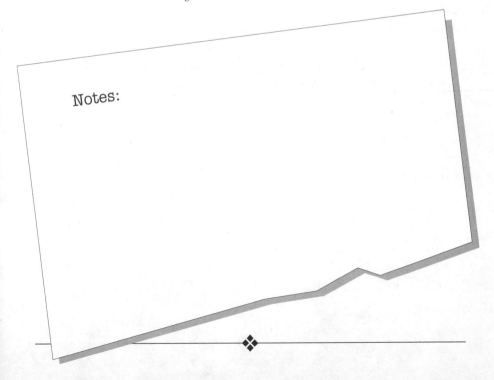

Notes:

SPAGO'S PECAN TART

The tart shell can be used with any filling, and the caramel sauce can be served over ice cream as well.

1 ½ cups light corn syrup
¾ cup granulated sugar
¾ cup brown sugar, packed
4 eggs plus 2 egg yolks
3 tablespoons unsalted butter
6 to 8 Tart Shells
1 ½ to 2 cups unbroken pecan halves
Caramel Sauce

Combine corn syrup, granulated and brown sugars, eggs and egg yolks in medium-sized bowl. (Save egg whites for another use.) Stir until blended. Heat butter in small skillet over medium heat until butter is foamy and light-brown in color. Remove from heat and whisk into corn syrup mixture. Set aside.

Arrange pastry shells on large baking sheet. Place pecans in tart shells and pour filling over (alternately, pour in filling, then arrange pecans in symmetrical pattern over filling). Bake at 375 degrees 35 to 40 minutes. Remove to wire rack to cool. Serve tarts at room temperature topped with Caramel Sauce. Makes 6 to 8 servings.

TART SHELLS

3 cups pastry flour
1 cup unsalted butter, very cold, cut into ½-inch pieces
3 tablespoons sugar
Dash salt
2 egg yolks
1 to 2 tablespoons whipping cream, very cold

Place flour, butter, sugar and salt in food processor. Process, using quick on-and-off motion, until mixture resembles coarse meal. Combine egg yolks (save egg whites for another use) and 1 tablespoon cream in small bowl. With processor motor running, add egg mixture. Process just until dough begins to form. Add enough remaining cream to form dough that holds together. Scrape dough onto piece of foil. Wrap airtight and refrigerate until well chilled, at least 1 hour.

Divide dough into 6 to 8 equal portions, depending upon whether pans are 3 or 4 inches.

Roll each portion out on lightly floured pastry cloth. Transfer pastry carefully to tart pans. Press against bottoms and sides of pans, then trim excess from rims. If pastry tears, patch with small bits of pastry trimmings. Reserve any remaining pastry, wrapped airtight, for another use. Makes 8 shells.

CARAMEL SAUCE

½ cup sugar, preferably vanilla sugar
⅔ cup whipping cream, at room temperature
2 tablespoons unsalted butter, at room temperature

Heat sugar in small, heavy skillet or saucepan over medium heat until melted and medium amber in color. Carefully pour in cream all at once, being careful to avoid splatters. Stir in butter.

Cook, stirring constantly, over medium heat until caramel dissolves and sauce is smooth. Remove from heat. Store at room temperature if not using immediately (sauce will harden when refrigerated). Makes about 1 cup.

❖

GREEN TOMATO PIE

What a wonderful way to use green tomatoes.

Pastry for double-crust pie
2 tablespoons flour
1 1/4 cups sugar
4 cups sliced green tomatoes
1/4 teaspoon salt
1/4 teaspoon ground cinnamon
1/4 cup lemon juice
1 tablespoon grated lemon peel
2 tablespoons butter or margarine

Roll out half of pastry and fit into 9-inch pie plate. Set aside. Mix flour and sugar. Sprinkle 1/4 of mixture into pie shell. Cover with tomato slices. Sprinkle with salt and top with remaining sugar mixture. Sprinkle cinnamon, lemon juice and peel evenly over top of pie. Dot with butter.

Roll out remaining pastry and cover pie with top crust. Make slits around pie dough. Bake at 450 degrees 10 minutes. Reduce heat and bake at 350 degrees 50 minutes longer. Makes 1 (9-inch) pie.

ODESSA'S SWEET POTATO PIE

This light and airy version of sweet potato pie from a reader uses whipping cream instead of the traditional evaporated milk.

1 ½ cups mashed cooked sweet potatoes
½ cup butter or margarine, softened
4 eggs
1 cup granulated or brown sugar
1 ½ teaspoons ground nutmeg
1 ½ teaspoons vanilla
Dash ground cinnamon
½ cup milk
1 unbaked 9-inch pastry shell

Blend sweet potatoes with butter. Add eggs, sugar, nutmeg, vanilla and cinnamon. Stir in milk. Let stand overnight in refrigerator to set slightly.

Turn into pastry shell and bake at 350 degrees 1½ hours. Cool. Makes 1 (9-inch) pie.

VIRGINIA DEPEW'S KENTUCKY BUTTERMILK PIE

Publicist Virginia Depew, who shared her grandmother's recipe, reported that her cousin found the handwritten recipe among the personal effects of her grandmother, who died at the age of 85 in 1938. "She had come to Kentucky as a young girl, when her family left Virginia, crossing the Pine Ridge Mountains," Depew said. "The Spradling women fed their menfolk sinfully rich desserts, resulting in costly dental problems in their later years." One taste and we understood.

3 ¾ cups sugar
½ cup flour
½ teaspoon salt
6 eggs
1 cup buttermilk
1 teaspoon vanilla
1 cup butter or margarine, melted
1 teaspoon butter extract (if using margarine), optional
2 (8-inch) unbaked pie shells or 1 (10-inch) unbaked pie shell

Mix sugar, flour and salt in bowl. Add eggs, stirring just enough to break up eggs. Add buttermilk and vanilla. Stir until just blended. Do not overbeat. Add melted butter. Stir slightly and quickly. Pour into pie shells and bake at 350 degrees 45 to 50 minutes, or until center of pie is set when shaken slightly. Cool thoroughly before cutting. (Pies may be frozen weeks or months before using. Allow 1 full day for thawing in refrigerator.) Makes 2 (8-inch) pies or 1 (10-inch) pie.

WOODY AND EDDY'S PEANUT BUTTER PIE

This recipe for peanut butter pie from Woody and Eddy's restaurant in Pasadena, can be frozen or served soft in all its creamy glory.

1 cup crunchy peanut butter
1 cup sugar
1 (8-ounce) package cream cheese
1 teaspoon vanilla
2 teaspoons melted butter
1 (8-ounce) package frozen whipped topping, thawed
Chocolate-Graham Cracker Crumb Crust
Shaved chocolate
Peanuts

Mix peanut butter, sugar, cream cheese, vanilla and butter thoroughly until creamy. Fold in whipped topping. Pour into Chocolate-Graham Cracker Crust. Refrigerate overnight.

Garnish pie with additional whipped topping, reserved chocolate-graham cracker crumbs, shaved chocolate or peanuts. Makes 1 (9-inch) pie.

CHOCOLATE-GRAHAM CRACKER CRUMB CRUST

2 cups graham cracker crumbs
¼ cup melted butter
2 ounces grated bar chocolate

Combine crumbs, butter and chocolate until well mixed. Reserve ¼ cup for garnish. Press remaining crumbs into bottom and sides of 9-inch pie plate. Chill.

❖

PUDDINGS & SOUFFLÉS

Readers love old-fashioned puddings, judging from the mountains of mail received for this type of dessert. Holiday season entertaining inspires requests for raspberry trifle, chocolate or mango mousse and flans. Requests for Depression Era puddings, such as blueberry pudding, rice pudding and tapioca are a sure sign of nostalgia and usually increase in times when the economy is in a slump. The soufflés found in this chapter include our most popular: chocolate soufflé from a Hollywood bistro and *Cold Persimmon Soufflé*, which readers love to prepare during the holidays.

Dear S.O.S.:
The Diplomat Pudding at Musso & Frank Grill in Hollywood brought back childhood memories of my grandmother preparing dainty dishes of this pudding. I would love the recipe for old time's sake.
— Darlene

Dear Darlene:
The Musso & Frank people were happy to answer this request for old time's sake.

BREAD PUDDINGS

DIPLOMAT PUDDING

Musso & Frank Grill, one of Hollywood's oldest restaurants, is well-known for its cooking and this outstanding old-time pudding.

4 eggs
½ cup sugar
3 cups milk
½ teaspoon vanilla extract
3 slices white bread, cubed
6 tablespoons raisins
2 tablespoons butter
¼ cup whipping cream, whipped to soft peaks

Beat eggs and sugar until light and creamy. Continue beating, adding milk and vanilla. In each of 6 (7-ounce) baking cups, place bread cubes, 1 tablespoon raisins and 1 teaspoon butter. Add milk mixture, filling ⅔ full. Place cups in baking pan on middle rack of oven. Add boiling water to baking pan, halfway up sides of cups. Bake at 350 degrees until set or until clean knife inserted near center of pudding comes out clean, 25 to 30 minutes. Invert pudding onto serving plate. Serve with whipped cream or other desired sauce. Makes 6 servings.

ELEANOR ROOSEVELT'S BLUEBERRY PUDDING

Blueberry pudding from former First Lady Eleanor Roosevelt initially appeared in print in 1973.

½ cup butter or margarine, softened
½ teaspoon ground cinnamon
1 (1-pound) loaf firm bread
1 (1-pound 5-ounce) can blueberry pie filling

Line 9 x 5-inch loaf pan with foil, letting ends extend over edge of pan. Combine butter and cinnamon. Trim crusts from bread and brush both sides of each slice with butter mixture.

Layer buttered bread and blueberry filling in pan, beginning and ending with bread, cutting slices to fit pan. Chill several hours.

Invert pan on platter. Carefully remove foil and cut pudding into slices. Makes 6 to 8 servings.

Note: Serve with Vanilla Custard (page 109) or Whipped Cream (page 168).

VINCENT PRICE'S BREAD PUDDING

Ever since the late actor, Vincent Price, shared his recipe for bread pudding with chef Bob Blakesly of Rancho Bernardo Inn in San Diego, Price's pudding has been on top of the dessert list.

¼ cup raisins
¼ cup brown sugar, packed
8 slices white bread
3 eggs, beaten
4 cups milk
1 ½ teaspoons vanilla
2 tablespoons unsalted butter, diced
Creme Anglaise

Sprinkle raisins and brown sugar evenly in well-buttered 13 x 9-inch glass baking dish. Line dish with bread slices. Set aside.

Combine eggs, milk and vanilla and pour over bread slices. Dot with butter.

Place baking dish in hot water bath. Bake at 350 degrees 1 hour or until pudding is firm. Serve in squares with Creme Anglaise. Makes 8 to 12 servings.

CREME ANGLAISE

6 egg yolks
¾ cup sugar
2 cups milk
Dash salt
1 teaspoon vanilla

Combine egg yolks and sugar. Mix thoroughly until smooth. Set aside.

Bring milk to simmer. Add salt and vanilla.

Combine egg mixture with small amount hot milk and return to milk mixture. Heat over low heat until thickened, stirring constantly. Strain and cool. Makes 2 cups.

❖

CUSTARDS

CITRUS CREME BRULEÉ

Michel Richard, chef-owner of the famed Citrus restaurant in Hollywood, sent us this extraordinarily rich creme bruleé recipe.

10 eggs, separated
¾ cup granulated sugar
¾ cup milk
2 ¼ cup whipping cream
1 tablespoon vanilla
¼ cup brown sugar, packed

Mix egg yolks and ½ cup sugar until well combined and sugar has dissolved. Add milk,
whipping cream and vanilla and mix well.

Place 1 9 x 13-inch glass baking dish or 6 (5-inch) fluted glass flan dishes in baking
pan. Pour mixture into baking dish or fill flan dishes ¾ full with creme bruleé mixture.
Place in oven in baking sheet ¾ full with hot water. Bake at 350 degrees 30 to 40 minutes
or until knife inserted near center comes out clean. Remove dishes from hot water bath
and set aside to cool.

Combine remaining ¼ cup granulated and brown sugar. Sprinkle top of each serving
evenly with combined sugars. Place creme bruleé in refrigerator until chilled. When ready
to serve, place sugar-coated creme in preheated boiler 5 minutes to brown, being careful
not to scorch. Makes 6 servings.

*Note: If using 9 x 13-inch baking dish, individual servings may be cut out with cookie
cutter for scalloped effect, if desired.*

❖

EL CHOLO FLAN

This scrumptious flan from El Cholo in Los Angeles can be varied by adding fruit as a garnish.

2 (15-ounce) cans sweetened condensed milk
2 cups milk
½ cup cream of coconut
½ cup corn syrup
1 teaspoon vanilla
6 eggs
1 cup sugar

Place sweetened condensed milk, milk, cream of coconut, corn syrup, vanilla and eggs in blender container. Blend thoroughly, or beat vigorously with wire whisk to blend well.

Melt sugar in heavy skillet over low heat, stirring occasionally to keep caramel from scorching. Add few drops of water little at time, stirring until caramel is of spreading consistency.

Distribute caramel evenly among 8 (4½- to 5-ounce) custard cups, tilting cups to spread caramel evenly. Or spread in 13 x 9-inch rectangular baking pan. Pour flan into caramel-lined cups or pan and place in shallow baking pan with ¼-inch hot water.

Cover with foil and bake cups at 350 degrees 50 minutes, or baking pan 60 minutes, or until firm. Cool, then place in refrigerator about 1 hour.

To serve, run knife around edges of cups or pan and invert on serving platter. Makes 8 servings.

FIVE CROWNS RASPBERRY TRIFLE

The rum pudding called for in this recipe is made with pudding mix, an excellent shortcut dessert to serve by itself.

1 (3 ¼-ounce) package vanilla pudding mix
2 cups half and half
2 tablespoons dark rum
2 ¼ cups whipping cream
3 tablespoons sugar
2 tablespoons red raspberry preserves
1 (10-inch) round spongecake layer, 2 inches thick
¼ cup brandy
¼ cup Sherry
30 to 38 whole strawberries

Combine pudding mix and half and half in saucepan. Cook over low heat until mixture comes to boil and partially thickens. Stir in rum, then chill pudding thoroughly.

Combine 1¼ cups whipping cream and 1 tablespoon sugar and whip until cream is stiff. Fold into chilled pudding mixture.

Using brush, coat deep 10-inch bowl with raspberry preserves to within 1 inch of top of bowl. Slice spongecake horizontally into quarters. Place top slice, crust side up, in bottom of coated bowl. Cut remaining slices into fingers, about 2 inches wide and stand against sides of bowl, pressing so fingers adhere to coating.

Combine brandy and Sherry and sprinkle over cake in bottom and on sides. Spoon custard into bowl. Beat remaining 1 cup whipping cream with 2 tablespoons sugar until stiff. Pipe whipped cream around rim of bowl and in mounds around center. Garnish with strawberries. Refrigerate at least 2 hours. To serve, spoon onto chilled dessert plates. Makes 6 to 8 servings.

FRIED MILK *(Leche Frita)*

Leche Frita is a cream pudding that is standard throughout Latin America. It's cut into squares and fried in butter.

2 cups milk
½ cup sugar
½ cup farina
2 eggs, beaten
½ teaspoon vanilla
Butter or margarine
Powdered sugar, optional

Combine milk, sugar, farina, eggs and vanilla in saucepan. Bring to boil, then cook and stir until mixture is paste consistency. Pour into 9-inch square pan. Cool, then cut into 2-inch squares.

Melt small amount of butter in skillet and fry squares until golden on both sides, adding more butter if needed to prevent sticking. Sprinkle with powdered sugar, if desired. Makes about 16 squares.

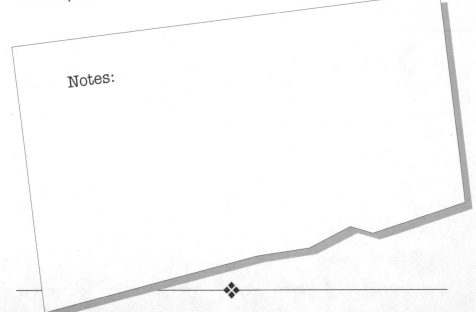

Notes:

FLOATING ISLANDS FROM XIOMARA

Patrick Healy, the consulting chef at Xiomara in Pasadena, California, forms these gorgeous Floating Islands into huge domes and tops them with a praline sauce.

1 ²/₃ cups egg whites (about 13 eggs)
3 ¹/₂ cups sugar
2 tablespoons water
Creme Anglaise

Beat egg whites (reserve egg yolks for another use) until soft peaks form. Gradually add 1½ cups sugar, beating constantly until sugar is well incorporated and whites are stiff but not dry.

Cut 8 (12-inch) squares of plastic wrap. Using pastry bag with no tip, pipe enough of egg-white mixture on top of each square to form grapefruit-size ball. Wrap corners of plastic wrap around egg-white mixture to form ball.

In large pan bring about 3 to 4 inches water to boil. Remove from heat and add floating islands. Cover and allow to steam about 10 minutes or until meringues are well puffed. Remove and let cool on flat surface. Refrigerate 24 hours.

Remove floating islands from plastic wrap and place on lightly oiled baking sheet or metal tray.

Place 2 cups sugar and 2 tablespoons water in saucepan and cook over medium-high heat until golden-brown caramel color. Spoon caramel over top of each floating island. Pour Creme Anglaise in serving bowl. Once caramel has hardened, remove floating islands. To serve, float each in bowl of Creme Anglaise. Makes 8 servings.

❖

CREME ANGLAISE

6 egg yolks
⅔ cup sugar
1 ½ cups hot milk
1 tablespoons vanilla
Praline Paste, optional
2 tablespoons whipping cream, whipped

Whisk egg yolks (reserve egg whites for another use) in saucepan, adding sugar by spoonfuls in rapid sequence. Do not add all at once or yolks will turn grainy. Continue beating 2 to 3 minutes until mixture is pale-yellow and thick. Add hot milk in thin stream, stirring (not beating) to avoid foaming.

Place saucepan over medium-low heat and stir with wooden spoon, being careful to stir over bottom and sides of pan. Sauce should gradually near simmer (but not simmer). Do not overheat or eggs will curdle. Heat only until egg mixture thickens, and surface bubbles begin to subside and steam rises. Sauce is done when coats back of wooden spoon thickly enough to hold line when finger is drawn across.

Strain sauce through fine mesh strainer to remove any cooked egg particles. Add vanilla. Sauce may be refrigerated in covered container several days.

Just before serving, whisk in desired flavor, such as praline paste, to taste. Sauce may also be flavored with caramel, coffee extract, Grand Marnier, Cointreau, rum or Cognac. Whisk in whipped cream to give sauce velvety texture.

PRALINE PASTE

1 cup pecans
Water

Blend pecans to form paste, using few drops of water to liquefy slightly.

LOS ANGELES TIMES CAFETERIA TAPIOCA

When readers request the recipe for tapioca pudding we send them this version from our own Los Angeles Times cafeteria.

1 quart milk
⅓ cup tapioca
2 eggs, separated
½ cup sugar
¼ teaspoon salt
1 ½ teaspoons vanilla
Whipped cream, optional
Maraschino cherries, optional

Heat milk until scalding. Stir in tapioca gradually. Cook mixture over boiling water or direct low heat 6 to 8 minutes until tapioca is done.

Beat egg yolks until pale in color. Beat with ¼ cup sugar and salt. Stir into tapioca. Cook and stir until mixture thickens slightly. Stir in vanilla. Cool slightly.

Beat egg whites and remaining ¼ cup sugar until stiff. Fold into hot pudding. Cool thoroughly, covered with wax paper.

To serve, spoon into dessert or parfait dishes. Garnish with whipped cream and maraschino cherry, if desired. Makes 12 (½-cup) servings.

❖

RUSSIAN CREAM

This delicate, old-fashioned gelatin cream dessert has had numerous revivals over the years.

1 envelope unflavored gelatin
¾ cup sugar
1 cup boiling water
1 cup whipping cream
1 cup sour cream
1 ½ teaspoons vanilla
Strawberries

Mix gelatin with sugar. Add boiling water and stir until gelatin is completely dissolved. Stir in whipping cream and chill until slightly thickened. Add sour cream and vanilla. Beat with rotary beater until mixture is bubbly.

Pour into 1-quart mold or individual molds. Chill until firm, at least 2 hours. Remove from mold and serve with whole strawberries or sliced or diced fresh fruit. Makes 4 servings.

Notes:

TIRAMISU

Chianti Cucina, a modern Italian restaurant in Los Angeles, was among the first in Los Angeles to feature this popular Italian trifle.

16 ladyfinger cookies or Italian biscotti
1 cup amaretto, rum or Frangelico
5 eggs, separated
1 ⅔ cups powdered sugar
8 ounces mascarpone cheese, softened
2 to 3 tablespoons unsweetened cocoa, sifted or coarsely grated
Bittersweet chocolate

Place ladyfinger cookies in bottom of shallow 8-cup rectangular or oval serving dish. Pour rum over ladyfinger to soak.

In large bowl, combine egg yolks and powdered sugar and beat with wire whisk or rotary beater until mixture turns pale yellow and forms a ribbon when beater is lifted. Carefully stir in mascarpone until completely incorporated.

With clean whisk or rotary beater, whip egg whites until stiff. Stir half of whites into mascarpone mixture to lighten. Gently but quickly fold in remaining whites.

Pour mixture over lady fingers and smooth with rubber spatula. Sprinkle with cocoa and refrigerate, covered, 1 to 2 hours. Serve from serving dish. Makes 6 to 8 servings.

Note: A creamy cheese, such as cream cheese or Mexican fresh cheese can be substituted for Italian mascarpone.

Note: See warning on the use of raw eggs, page 256.

❖

WAYSIDE INN BAKED INDIAN PUDDING

Chef Steve Pickford of the Wayside Inn sent us this traditional New England pudding recipe that recalls the winter holidays.

5 ¼ cups milk
¾ cup cornmeal
1 cup molasses
½ teaspoon salt
½ teaspoon cinnamon
½ teaspoon nutmeg
½ teaspoon ginger
3 eggs

Bring 4 cups milk to boil in heavy saucepan. Add cornmeal to milk and beat with wire whisk until thickened. Add molasses, salt, cinnamon, nutmeg and ginger and return to boil.

In separate bowl, blend together 1¼ cups milk and eggs. Add.to hot mixture and stir to mix well. Mixture may appear curdled.

Turn into buttered and sugared 2-quart casserole. Bake at 350 degrees 1 hour. Knife inserted near center should come out clean when done. Let stand 30 minutes before serving. Makes 8 to 10 servings.

GELATIN

ESPRESSO COFFEE JELLY

Japanese-French restaurant chefs first served coffee jelly as dessert to Los Angeles patrons in the early '70s.

> 2 envelopes unflavored gelatin
> 1/2 cup water
> 3 cups strong espresso coffee
> 2 sticks cinnamon, optional
> 3 whole cloves, optional
> 2/3 cup sugar
> Dash salt
> 1/4 cup rum
> Whipped cream (Page 168)
> Chocolate curls

Soften gelatin in cold water. Combine espresso coffee with cinnamon and cloves in saucepan, if desired. Bring to boil, reduce heat and simmer 5 minutes. Remove cinnamon and cloves. Add gelatin and stir until dissolved. Stir in sugar, salt and rum. Pour into demitasse cups, dessert dishes or 1-quart mold. Chill until firm. If using mold, unmold onto serving platter. Garnish jelly with whipped cream and chocolate curls. Makes 8 servings.

Note: To make chocolate curls using potato peeler, scrap edges of room temperature chocolate bar over wax paper. Refrigerate until ready to use.

❖

MOUSSE

CHOCOLATE MOUSSE SANGLIER

The Times' Sunday Home magazine first featured this recipe for Chocolate Mousse Sanglier in the '70s and it has been popular since.

⅓ cup sugar minus 1 tablespoon
¼ cup water
2 egg whites, at room temperature
1 cup semisweet chocolate pieces
¼ cup rum
3 cups whipping cream

Place sugar in saucepan with water and cook just to point when syrup barely turns pale golden color or just before mixture begins to caramelize. Beat egg whites until foamy, and gradually add sugar syrup, beating constantly.

Melt chocolate with rum and fold into sugar mixture. Cool 2 hours in refrigerator.

Whip cream and fold into chocolate mixture. Spoon into serving dishes, demitasse or stemmed glasses. Makes 8 servings.

CRANBERRY MOUSSE

Cranberry Mousse using whole cranberry sauce, raspberry gelatin and whipped topping is popular because it so easy to assemble and can be prepared well ahead of time.

1 (3-ounce) package raspberry gelatin
1 cup orange juice
¼ cup sugar
⅛ teaspoon salt
1 cup whole cranberry sauce
1 cup nondairy whipped topping
½ cup slivered almonds, optional

Combine gelatin, orange juice, sugar and salt in saucepan. Heat and stir until gelatin is dissolved. Fold in cranberry sauce and chill until mixture is thickened slightly.

Fold in whipped topping. Turn into dessert bowl and chill until set. Garnish with almonds. Makes 4 to 6 servings.

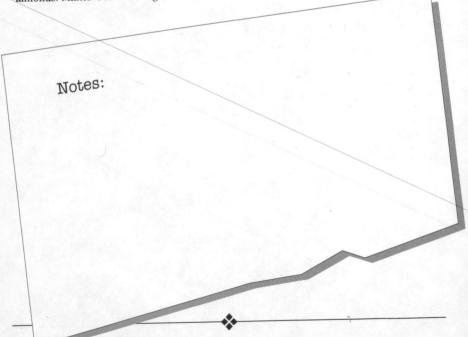

Notes:

EL TORITO KAHLUA MOUSSE

The Kahlua Mousse recipe appeared in an El Torito Restaurant and Cantina brochure of favorite recipes.

2 cups nondairy whipped topping
½ cup whipping cream
1 tablespoon instant coffee
2 tablespoons unsweetened cocoa powder
3 tablespoons sugar
6 tablespoons Kahlua liqueur
Additional whipped cream
Chocolate sprinkles
Wafer cookies

Beat nondairy whipped topping and whipping cream until stiff peaks form. Add coffee, cocoa and sugar, blending well. Add Kahlua, stirring mixture with rubber spatula. Chill in refrigerator.

When ready to serve, top mousse with additional whipped cream, chocolate sprinkles and serve with wafer cookies. Makes 8 servings.

VANILLA RUM MOUSSE

This mousse from Gulliver's in Irvine, California, has been a Times favorite for years.

1 cup whipping cream
¼ cup sugar
Pastry Cream
2 ounces dark rum
Melba Sauce
Additional whipped cream

Whip cream with sugar until stiff. Blend Pastry Cream and rum until smooth. Fold whipped cream into Pastry Cream. Place 2 tablespoons Melba Sauce in bottom of each of 4 (4-ounce) wine glasses. Pipe or spoon mousse on top so sauce travels halfway up glass. Top with additional Melba Sauce and garnish with whipped cream. Makes 4 servings.

PASTRY CREAM

½ cup sugar
3 ½ tablespoons cornstarch
½ teaspoon salt
1 ½ cups milk
2 eggs, lightly beaten
1 tablespoon butter or margarine
1 teaspoon vanilla

Combine sugar, cornstarch and salt and blend with ½ cup cold milk. Scald remaining 1 cup milk in top of double boiler over low heat and add sugar mixture, stirring constantly.

Place mixture over simmering water and cook, stirring, until thickened. Cover and cook 20 minutes, stirring occasionally. Pour small amount of hot mixture into eggs, stirring constantly. Combine eggs with remaining hot mixture and cook 10 minutes, stirring constantly. Remove custard from heat and add butter. Cool slightly and add vanilla. Makes 1½ cups.

MELBA SAUCE

1 (10-ounce) package frozen raspberries
½ cup sugar
½ cup strawberry jelly
1 tablespoon cornstarch
1 tablespoon water

Thaw frozen berries and mash. Combine with sugar in saucepan. Add jelly and cook over low heat until mixture comes to boil.

Combine cornstarch and water and add to berry mixture. Cook, stirring, until sauce is clear and slightly thickened. Cool. Makes 1 cup.

VARIATION:
SHORT CUT VANILLA RUM MOUSSE
Substitute 1 (3-ounce) package vanilla pudding mix, prepared according to manufacturer's directions, for Pastry Cream recipe.

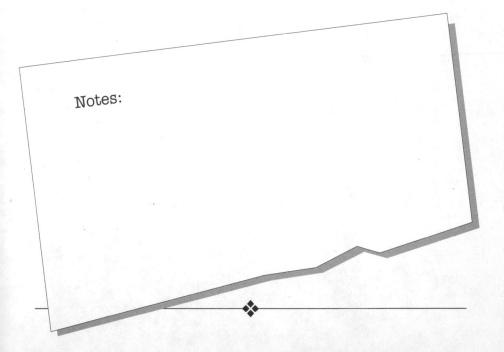

Notes:

MANGO MOUSSE

Mango Mousse can be enjoyed year-round.

1 tablespoon unflavored gelatin
¼ cup water
2 cups fresh mango pulp or any fresh pureed fruit
½ cup sugar
2 tablespoons fruit-flavored liqueur
2 tablespoons lemon juice
1 cup whipping cream, chilled and whipped
2 egg whites, beaten stiff

Soften gelatin in water. Puree mango pulp. Add sugar, liqueur, gelatin mixture and lemon juice. Blend until smooth.

Fold in whipped cream and refrigerate about 1 hour or just until mixture begins to set. Fold in egg whites until no lumps remain.

Spoon or pipe mousse into demitasse or tea cups or individual serving bowls, piling high. Refrigerate until ready to use. Makes 4 to 6 servings.

Note: See warning on the use of raw eggs, page 256.

RICE PUDDINGS

Chocolate Rice Pudding

Mouths water at the sight of this Chocolate Rice Pudding with a hard sauce of butter and brown sugar over the warm pudding.

> *2 cups milk*
> *½ cup sugar*
> *¼ cup butter*
> *2 squares unsweetened chocolate*
> *1 teaspoon vanilla extract*
> *¼ teaspoon salt*
> *½ cup rice*
> *Hard Sauce, optional*
> *Whipped Cream (Page 168), optional*

Cook milk, sugar, butter, chocolate, vanilla extract and salt in saucepan over medium heat, stirring, just until tiny bubbles appear around edges. Stir in rice. Cover and simmer over low heat, stirring often, about 1 hour. Serve hot with Hard Sauce or whipped cream.

> **HARD SAUCE**
>
> *½ cup butter or margarine*
> *2 cup powdered sugar*
> *Brandy or rum*
> *Dash each nutmeg and cinnamon*

Melt butter and stir in sugar. Add brandy or rum until mixture can be stirred. Add nutmeg and cinnamon. Whip with fork before serving.

CLIFTON'S RICE CUSTARD

Rice pudding from Clifton's Cafeteria in West Covina has became a standard favorite.

4 eggs, slightly beaten
½ cup sugar
⅔ teaspoon mace
¼ teaspoon salt
3 cups milk
1 teaspoon vanilla
1 ⅓ cups cooked rice

Blend eggs, sugar, mace and salt. Add milk to egg mixture and mix well. Stir in vanilla. Place cooked rice in 8-inch square pan. Pour milk mixture over rice, filling pan to within ½ inch of top.

Place pan in larger pan and add hot water to about halfway up pudding pan. Bake at 400 degrees 35 to 40 minutes or until knife inserted in center comes out clean. Cut into squares to serve. Makes 9 servings.

DOUBLE BOILER RICE PUDDING

If you don't have a double boiler use two saucepans, the larger to contain water and the smaller pan to hold the ingredients.

½ cup uncooked rice
3 cups boiling water
½ teaspoon salt
1 (15-ounce) can sweetened condensed milk
¼ cup butter or margarine
½ cup raisins
1 teaspoon vanilla

Measure rice, boiling water and salt into top of double boiler. Cook over rapidly boiling water until rice is tender, about 40 minutes. Stir in sweetened condensed milk, butter and raisins. Cook, stirring frequently, until slightly thickened, about 20 minutes. Remove from heat and stir in vanilla. Serve warm or cold. Makes 8 servings.

HAYDEN'S RICE PUDDING

A stove-top, long-cooking rice pudding, produced a controversy when some readers believed it to have originated from Hayden's in Desert Hot Springs while others attributed the recipe to actor Sterling Hayden well before his death in 1986.

1 cup boiling water
½ cup long grain rice
½ teaspoon salt (or less to taste)
1 quart milk
¼ cup butter
2 eggs
½ cup sugar
1 teaspoon vanilla
½ cup raisins
Cinnamon-sugar or nutmeg

Combine boiling water, rice and salt in saucepan. Bring to boil again and cook 7 minutes. Add milk and butter. Bring to boil again, then reduce heat and simmer, covered, 1¼ hours. Beat eggs with sugar and vanilla and add to cooked rice mixture. Remove from heat and add raisins. Turn into shallow buttered pan and sprinkle with cinnamon-sugar or nutmeg. Cover with plastic wrap and chill thoroughly before serving. Makes 4 to 6 servings.

❖

HEAVENLY HASH

This fruit-filled rice pudding made with leftover cold, cooked rice, dates back to the '40s when it was a popular ladies club luncheon dessert.

> *2 cups cold cooked rice*
> *1 (8¾-ounce) can pineapple tidbits or crushed pineapple*
> *¼ cup sliced maraschino cherries*
> *1 cup miniature marshmallows*
> *Dash salt*
> *1 cup whipping cream*

Lightly mix rice, drained pineapple, cherries, marshmallows and salt. Chill well. Just before serving, whip cream and fold into rice mixture. Pile into dessert dishes and top with additional cherries, if desired. Makes 6 servings.

Notes:

OLD WORLD RICE PUDDING

Old World Restaurant in Westwood, California, has been serving this rice pudding to UCLA students for decades.

2 whole eggs
2 egg yolks
½ cup sugar
Dash salt
Dash cinnamon
1 teaspoon vanilla
1 quart milk
Butter
½ cup cooked rice
½ cup raisins
Ground nutmeg
Whipped Cream

Combine eggs, egg yolks, sugar, salt, cinnamon and vanilla in mixing bowl. Mix well.
Heat milk in saucepan. Pour in egg mixture, stirring.
Lightly butter 6 individual bowls or 1½-quart soufflé dish. Place rice and raisins in bottom of bowls. Pour egg mixture over rice mixture. Sprinkle with nutmeg to taste.
Stirring every 20 minutes, bake at 350 degrees 1½ hours for large pudding, or 30 to 40 minutes for individual dishes. Serve warm or cold, with or without whipped cream. Makes 6 servings. Serve warm or cold, with or without whipped cream.

WHIPPED CREAM

⅓ cup heavy whipping cream
½ teaspoon vanilla
1 tablespoon powdered sugar

In bowl, whip cream with vanilla and sugar until stiff.

❖

SOUFFLÉS

COLD LEMON SOUFFLÉ

This cold lemon soufflé is ideal when you'd like a dessert that can be made well ahead of time.

> **3 envelopes unflavored gelatin**
> **1 ½ cups sugar**
> **9 eggs, separated**
> **1 cup plus 2 tablespoons lemon juice**
> **¾ cup water**
> **3 tablespoons grated lemon peel**
> **¾ teaspoon salt**
> **Additional lemon peel and sugar**

Mix gelatin and ¾ cup sugar in top of double boiler. Add slightly beaten egg yolks, lemon juice and water to gelatin mixture. Cook and stir over simmering water until gelatin dissolves and mixture thickens slightly. Add lemon peel and remove from heat. Chill, stirring occasionally, until mixture begins to set. Add salt to egg whites and beat until soft peaks form. Gradually add remaining ¾ cup sugar, beating until stiff, glossy peaks form. Gently fold in gelatin mixture. Pour into lightly oiled 1-quart soufflé dish with a 4-inch oiled collar. Chill 3 to 4 hours. Carefully remove collar. Mix lemon peel with a small amount of sugar and pat mixture onto collar. Garnish top with a lemon slice. Makes 6 to 8 servings.

Note: To make a paper collar, fold a strip of wax paper 4-inches deep long enough to overlap 6- to 8-inch soufflé dish when wrapped around. Place around soufflé dish to come 2 inches up from rim. Tie with string to secure tightly. (Collar is discarded after soufflé is firm enough to hold its shape.)

Note: See warning on the use of raw eggs, page 256.

COLD PERSIMMON SOUFFLÉ

Requests for Cold Persimmon Soufflé arrive at the brink of the Christmas season without fail.

2 envelopes unflavored gelatin
¼ cup water
4 eggs
⅔ cup sugar
1 ½ cup pureed persimmon pulp
¼ cup orange curacao
1 teaspoon vanilla
1 cup whipping cream, whipped
¼ cup chopped or sliced almonds, lightly toasted

Sprinkle gelatin over water to soften. Heat over low heat to dissolve gelatin. Beat eggs thoroughly in bowl. Gradually add sugar and continue to beat until mixture is smooth and very thick. Fold in gelatin. Stir in persimmon, curacao and vanilla. Fold in whipped cream. Turn into soufflé dish and sprinkle almonds evenly over top. Chill until firm. Makes 6 servings.

Note: See warning on use of raw eggs, page 256.

Notes:

MOUSTACHE CAFE CHOCOLATE SOUFFLÉ

Readers long to re-create Hollywood's Moustache Cafe's chocolate soufflé to serve at home.

7 ounces dark unsweetened chocolate
½ cup milk
Granulated sugar
4 egg yolks
6 egg whites
Butter
Powdered sugar
Whipped cream, optional

Combine unsweetened chocolate, milk and 7 tablespoons granulated sugar in top of double boiler over simmering water. Cook, stirring occasionally, until chocolate and sugar are melted. Remove from heat. Let stand 10 minutes.

Drop egg yolks into chocolate mixture. Using wire whisk, mix until blended.

Beat egg whites with mixer until stiff. Add 1 tablespoon granulated sugar and continue beating until blended. Using wire whisk, add ⅓ of egg white mixture to chocolate mixture and whip until blended. Gently fold remaining egg whites into mixture.

Butter 6 individual soufflé dishes, covering entire inside surface and rim. Sprinkle with granulated sugar to taste.

Fill each soufflé dish to rim with chocolate mixture. Bake 20 minutes at 350 degrees. Remove from oven. Dust with powdered sugar to taste. Serve at once with dollop of whipped cream. Makes 6 servings.

❖

STRAWBERRY SOUFFLÉ

The recipe for Strawberry Soufflé appeared in the Home magazine section of The Times in 1980 and has been reprinted often by reader demand.

2 envelopes unflavored gelatin
1 cup cold water
1 cup sugar
1 quart strawberries, washed and hulled
1 tablespoon lemon juice
1 teaspoon vanilla
5 egg whites
1 cup whipping cream, whipped

Sprinkle gelatin evenly over cold water in saucepan. Place over low heat and stir gently until gelatin is dissolved. Remove from heat and add ⅔ cup sugar. Stir until dissolved.

Mash or puree berries in food processor or blender. Add to gelatin with lemon juice and vanilla. Chill, stirring occasionally, until mixture mounds slightly from spoon.

Remove from refrigerator. Beat egg whites until soft peaks form. Gradually add remaining ⅓ cup sugar and continue to beat until stiff peaks are formed. Fold into berry mixture. Fold in whipped cream.

Pour berry mixture into 6 to 8-cup soufflé mold with 4-inch collar (see note on page 169). Chill until firm, several hours or overnight.

Before serving, carefully peel off paper collar. Garnish with additional whipped cream, whole strawberries and leaves, if desired. Makes 6 to 8 servings.

Note: See warning on use of raw eggs, page 256.

❖

STEAMED PUDDINGS

FIGGY PUDDING

Young readers often ask if there really is a "Figgy Pudding," as referred to in the Christmas carol.

⅓ cup shortening
⅔ cup sugar
2 eggs, beaten
1 cup chopped dried figs
⅓ cup diced candied orange peel
¼ cup finely chopped citron
½ cup chopped nuts
½ teaspoon salt
2 teaspoons baking powder
4 cups graham cracker crumbs
1 cup milk
Hard Sauce (Page 163), optional

Cream together shortening and sugar. Add eggs and mix well. stir in figs, orange peel, citron and nuts. Combine salt, baking powder and crumbs. Add alternately with milk to fruit mixture. Turn into greased 6-cup mold, cover and steam 3 hours. Unmold. Can be served with Hard Sauce. Makes 10 to 12 servings.

❖

ENGLISH-STYLE PLUM PUDDING

Here's a typical English-style plum pudding readers ask us to print every Christmas.

1 cup flour
½ teaspoon each cinnamon, cloves and allspice
½ teaspoon salt
½ cup each ground or finely chopped raisins, dates and nuts
¼ cup finely chopped mixed candied fruit
½ cup milk
1 cup soft bread crumbs
2 eggs, beaten
½ cup sugar
½ cup ground suet
½ teaspoon soda
⅓ cup hot water
Hard Sauce (Page 163)

Sift together flour, spices and salt. Mix in ground raisins, dates and nuts and chopped fruit. Pour milk over bread crumbs. Mix in eggs, sugar and suet. Add soda, dissolved in hot water, and blend into bread crumbs. Combine fruit and bread crumb mixtures. Turn into well-greased 1-quart mold, cover and place on rack in steamer. Cover and steam over 1 inch boiling water 3 hours, adding more water as needed. Place on rack to cool slightly, turn out and serve with Hard Sauce. Makes 8 servings.

❖

PERSIMMON PECAN PUDDING

Here is a version of a popular persimmon steamed pudding made with pecans.

½ cup granulated sugar
½ cup brown sugar, packed
½ cup melted butter
¼ teaspoon salt
¼ teaspoon EACH cinnamon and nutmeg
1 cup flour, sifted
1 cup puréed persimmon (3 to 4 very ripe fruit)
2 teaspoons baking soda
2 teaspoons warm water
¼ cup brandy
1 teaspoon vanilla
2 eggs, lightly beaten
½ cup chopped pecans, walnuts or almonds
1 cup raisins, optional
Hard Sauce (Page 163)

Combine granulated and brown sugars in large bowl. Add melted butter, stirring to mix well. Add salt, cinnamon and nutmeg to flour and resift. Add to sugar-butter mixture. Stir in persimmon pulp, mixing well. Dissolve baking soda in warm water. Add to persimmon mixture. Stir in brandy and vanilla. Add eggs and mix well. Add pecans and raisins, if desired, stirring to mix well.

Turn batter into well-buttered 5- to 6-cup heat-proof pudding mold. Cover tightly and place on rack in kettle. Pour enough boiling water into kettle to reach halfway up sides of mold. Cover kettle and simmer 2½ to 3 hours. Let stand afew minutes before unmolding.

Unmold onto serving dish and serve with Hard Sauce or Whipped Cream (Page 168) flavored with brandy extract, if desired. Makes 6 to 8 servings.

❖

FROZEN DESSERTS

A dessert in the freezer saves a busy host from last-minute hassle. You simply make the dessert ahead and forget it until you are ready to serve. Some of the most popular frozen desserts are so easy, yet glamorous, readers request them constantly. *Brandy Alexander Pie*, *Fried Ice Cream*, *Lemon Velvet* and *Peanut Butter Pie* are some of the top favorites in this chapter. Check "Dear S.O.S.," printed previously, for additional favorites not printed here.

Dear S.O.S.:
    We love the Fried Ice Cream found in Mexican restaurants, but don't have a clue as to how to prevent the ice cream ball from melting.
    – Mrs. D.D.

Dear Mrs. D.D.:
    The trick is to insulate the cookie-coated ice cream ball well with beaten egg before frying.

CAKES

BAKED ALASKA

Old-fashioned as Baked Alaska may be, it makes periodic comebacks.

1 (9-inch) spongecake layer
1 quart brick ice cream (any flavor)
6 egg whites
½ teaspoon cream of tartar
1 cup sugar

Trim cake to 5 x 6-inch brick, reserving trimmings for another use. This size will fit half of ½-gallon brick of ice cream, which is easier to find than 1-quart bricks. Cut ice cream, if necessary, and freeze until very hard.

Place strip of heavy paper down center of board with ends of paper extending over edges of board. Place rectangle of cake on paper on board, then place ice cream brick on cake. Return to freezer until ice cream is very hard and until ready to serve.

Just before serving, beat egg whites with cream of tartar until soft peaks form. Gradually add sugar, beating until sugar is thoroughly dissolved and until very stiff peaks form. Working quickly, spread meringue over entire cake and ice cream, making sure there are no crevices in meringue to bottom of cake.

Bake at 475 degrees 3 minutes or until meringue is lightly tipped with brown. Serve from board or slip Alaska from board onto platter. Slice and serve at once. Makes 6 servings.

VARIATION:
FLAMING ALASKA
To flame, slip Baked Alaska off onto serving platter. Pour ¼ cup warmed brandy around Alaska and ignite. *Warning:* Be careful to keep loose clothing, hair, face and hands away from flame. Allow flame to go out. Slice to serve.

FROZEN CHOCOLATE CUPCAKES

This frozen chocolate dessert prepared in muffin cups was shared by a working mom for kids who loved to dabble in the kitchen.

4 squares unsweetened chocolate
1 cup butter or margarine, softened
2 cups sifted powdered sugar
4 eggs
¼ teaspoon peppermint flavoring
2 teaspoons vanilla extract
1 cup vanilla wafer or graham cracker crumbs
Whipped cream
Maraschino cherries

Melt chocolate in pan over hot water.

Beat together butter and powdered sugar until light and fluffy. Add melted chocolate and continue beating until smooth. Add eggs and blend well. Add peppermint and vanilla and beat until well blended.

Place cupcake papers in muffin tins. Cover bottom of each cup with some of cookie crumbs. Spoon in dessert. Top with remaining crumbs and freeze. When ready to serve, peel off paper. Top each with whipped cream and cherry. Makes 2 dozen cupcakes.

Note: See warning on use of raw eggs, page 256.

FRUIT

FROZEN FRUIT DESSERT (OR SALAD)

A traditional luncheon salad that doubles as dessert goes back to the '40s and '50s, when refrigerator-freezers emerged on the scene.

2 tablespoons sugar
1 tablespoon flour
½ cup honey
¼ cup lemon juice
1 egg, beaten
1 cup sliced dried figs
½ cup flake coconut
1 (11-ounce) can mandarin oranges, drained
1 cup whipping cream

Combine sugar, flour and honey. Bring to boil. Stir lemon juice into egg, then into honey mixture. Heat to boiling, stirring constantly. Remove from heat. Cool.

Stir in figs, coconut and oranges. Whip cream and fold into fruit mixture. Pour into refrigerator tray or individual molds. Freeze until firm. Makes about 8 servings.

Notes:

ICE CREAMS

BANANA SPLIT SUNDAE

An all-out banana split improvisation topped with "the works"—berries, whipped cream, fudge, butterscotch, nuts and fudge sauce—is from Ivy at the Shore in Santa Monica.

1 banana, split
Praline ice cream
Vanilla ice cream, preferably made with Tahitian vanilla
Chopped pineapple
Raspberries
Blueberries
Chopped strawberries
Blackberries
Mint leaves
Whipped cream
Butterscotch sauce
Chocolate fudge sauce
Toasted whole or coarsely chopped almonds

Place banana in oval serving dish. Top with total of 3 scoops praline and vanilla ice creams. Surround ice creams with desired amounts of pineapple, raspberries, blueberries, strawberries, and blackberries. Garnish with mint leaves. Serve with whipped cream, butterscotch sauce, fudge sauce and almonds placed on the side. Makes 1 to 2 servings.

EASY FROZEN YOGURT

You can add some cocoa powder to this recipe for frozen yogurt or use any fruit-flavored, ready-to-eat yogurt for a change of pace.

> *2 (8-ounce) cartons vanilla yogurt*
> *¼ cup light corn syrup*
> *2 tablespoons sugar*

In medium bowl stir together yogurt, corn syrup and sugar. Pour into 9x5-inch loaf pan. Cover with foil. Freeze until firm. Turn into blender container. Blend at medium speed 1 minute, or until liquefied.

Return to loaf pan. Cover and freeze until firm. Allow to stand at room temperature 10 minutes before serving. Makes about 1 pint, about 4 servings.

VARIATION:
MOCHA FROZEN YOGURT

For Mocha Frozen Yogurt follow basic recipe but substitute 2 (8-ounce) cartons coffee yogurt for vanilla yogurt. Add 1 tablespoon unsweetened cocoa powder. If coffee yogurt is not available, substitute vanilla yogurt and 2 teaspoons instant coffee granules.

FRIED ICE CREAM

Fried Ice Cream with a crunchy topping has been a reader favorite since the dessert was first featured as a specialty dessert in Mexican restaurants two decades ago.

1 pint vanilla or other flavor ice cream
1 ½ cups crushed corn flakes or cookie crumbs
1 teaspoon ground cinnamon
2 teaspoons sugar
1 egg
Oil for deep frying
Honey
Whipped cream

Scoop out 4 or 5 balls of ice cream. Place on plate and return to freezer. Mix corn flake crumbs, cinnamon and sugar in shallow bowl. Roll frozen ice cream balls in crumb mixture and freeze again. Beat egg and dip coated balls in egg, then roll again in remaining crumbs. Freeze until ready to use. (For thicker coating, repeat dipping in egg and rolling in crumbs.)

When ready to serve, heat oil to 350 degrees. Place 1 frozen ice cream ball in fryer basket or on slotted spoon and lower into hot oil 1 minute. Immediately remove and place in chilled dessert dish. Drizzle with honey and dollop with whipped cream.

Serve immediately or keep in freezer while continuing to fry remaining balls, one at time. Balls will be crunchy on the outside and just beginning to melt inside. Makes 4 to 5 servings.

LEMON VELVET

The recipe for Lemon Velvet first appeared in The Times in the 1960s, but goes back to the '40s when ice boxes gave way to refrigerators with freezer compartments.

1 3/4 cups sugar
Grated zest and juice of 3 to 4 lemons
2 cups half and half
1 (12 1/2 ounce) can evaporated milk
1 1/2 cups whole milk
Dash salt

Measure sugar into 1-gallon ice cream freezer can. Add lemon zest and juice. Stir in half and half and evaporated milk until smooth. Stir in enough whole milk to fill can 2/3 full. Add salt, if desired. Freeze according to manufacturer's directions. Makes 1 1/2 quarts, about 8 servings.

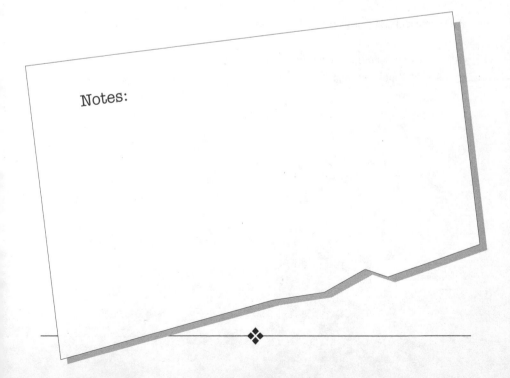

Notes:

❖

TORTONI

You can freeze Tortoni in a mold or individual cups to have on hand for snacks or serve at any planned or impromptu party occasion.

> *1 (14-ounce) can sweetened condensed milk*
> *3 egg yolks, beaten*
> *¼ cup light rum*
> *2 teaspoons vanilla*
> *⅔ cup coconut macaroon crumbs*
> *½ to ¾ cup toasted slivered almonds*
> *⅓ cup chopped maraschino cherries*
> *2 cups whipping cream, whipped*
> *Additional maraschino cherries*
> *Additional toasted slivered almonds*

Combine condensed milk, egg yolks, rum, vanilla, macaroon crumbs, slivered almonds and chopped cherries. Mix well. Fold in whipped cream.

Pour into lightly greased 2-quart ring mold or 12 individual, small paper cups. Cover with foil. Freeze 6 hours or until firm. If using ring mold, unmold Tortoni, using hot cloth on outside of mold to loosen, onto serving plate. Garnish with cherries and almonds. Makes 12 servings.

Note: See warning on the use of raw eggs, page 256.

POPS AND ICES

CHAMPAGNE POPS

These Champagne Pops were served in place of champagne as guests arrived at an outdoor celebrity party.

½ cup ginger ale
1 cup champagne
Twist of lime or lemon

Slowly add ginger ale to champagne. Add twist of lime and pour into ice tray with compartments that are easily loosened or removed. Freeze until mushy. Insert wooden skewer in center of each compartment and freeze several hours or overnight. Remove cubes from ice tray and place over a bed of ice to serve. Pass with napkins or paper cups to catch drips. Serve at once. Makes 12 to 14 pops.

VARIATION:
MIMOSA POPS
Use ½ cup orange juice in place of ginger ale in recipe for Champagne Pops.

FROZEN CHOCOLATE-BANANA POPS

Here's a nutritious snack children of all ages seem to enjoy.

6 firm ripe bananas
Chocolate Topping
Colored sprinkles, grated coconut or coarsely ground nuts

Cut peeled bananas in halves crosswise. Impale each half on wooden skewer and place in freezer 1 hour or until frozen. (Chocolate coating will run off if fruit is at room temperature.)

Remove bananas from freezer 1 at time. Dip and roll bananas in melted Chocolate Topping, making sure all banana surfaces are completely covered. Shake or twirl banana before removing from pan to remove excess coating. While coating is still soft, roll the covered banana in colored sprinkles, coconut or nuts. If coating becomes too hard to hold decorations, apply little warm coating to the pop.

When covering sets, place pops on squares of foil, wrap securely and store in freezer until ready to eat. Makes 12 pops.

CHOCOLATE TOPPING

1 (12-ounce) package semisweet chocolate pieces
6 tablespoons oil

Melt chocolate in top of double boiler over hot, not boiling, water. Add oil and stir until smooth. Keep warm over hot water while dipping. Makes enough topping to cover 12 pops.

❖

JUICIPOPS

Readers often request recipes for frozen fruit bars, especially pineapple-flavored ones.

1 ½ cup pineapple or orange juice
¼ cup undiluted orange juice concentrate
½ cup crushed pineapple or 1 ripe banana or 4 strawberries
¼ cup yogurt

Combine juice, orange juice concentrate, fruit and yogurt in blender container. Blend until smooth. Fill pop molds or ice cube trays with mixture. Freeze until firm. Makes 8 pops.

PIES

FABULOUS FROZEN BRANDY ALEXANDER PIE

This great hot weather pie was reprinted numerous times since its first appearance in 1977.

1 (14-ounce) can sweetened condensed milk
1 cup whipping cream, whipped
2 tablespoons creme de cacao
2 tablespoon brandy
1 (9-inch) graham cracker crust
Shaved chocolate for garnish, optional

In large bowl, combine sweetened condensed milk, whipped cream, creme de cacao and brandy. Pour into prepared crust. Freeze 4 to 6 hours or until firm. Garnish with shaved chocolate, if desired. Makes 6 servings.

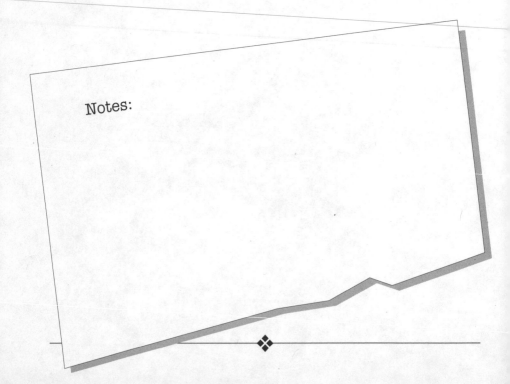

Notes:

NAUGHTY HULA PIE

The high number of calories in Naughty Hula Pie from El Crab Catcher at the Whaler's Village on Maui does not stop readers from repeatedly asking for this Hawaiian version of mud pie.

Chocolate Cookie Crumb Shell
1 quart macadamia nut ice cream
1 (8-ounce) jar hot fudge sauce
½ cup whipping cream, whipped
½ cup chopped macadamia nuts

Fill Chocolate Cookie Crumb Shell with ice cream. Level top with knife and return pie to freezer to freeze firm.

When ready to serve, remove from freezer and top with hot fudge sauce. Dollop with whipped cream and sprinkle with macadamia nuts. Makes 1 (9-inch) deep dish pie.

Note: If macadamia ice cream is unavailable, substitute 1 quart softened vanilla ice cream mixed with 1 (7-ounce) jar coarsely chopped macadamia nuts. Freeze, then pack into pie shell.

CHOCOLATE COOKIE CRUMB SHELL

2 cups cream-filled chocolate cookie crumbs (29 to 30 cookies)
½ cup sugar
½ cup butter or margarine, melted

Mix together cookie crumbs, sugar and butter. Mix, then pat onto bottom and sides of 9-inch deep pie dish. (Pie shell should be 3 inches deep.) Freeze 15 minutes.

❖

REESE'S FROZEN PEANUT BUTTER PIE

Reese's Country Inn in Niagara Falls, Ontario, serves this peanut butter pie that has become popular with readers.

2 ³⁄₄ pints vanilla ice cream
¹⁄₂ cup peanut butter
2 ounces semisweet chocolate pieces
Cocoa-Graham Cracker Crust
Chocolate Sauce
Sweetened whipped cream

Stir vanilla ice cream with peanut butter and chocolate pieces by hand. Spoon into Cocoa-Graham Cracker Crust. Freeze immediately until solid, about 2 hours or overnight. Top with Chocolate Sauce and whipped cream. Makes 8 servings.

Note: Do not allow ice cream to become too soft before mixing with peanut butter. If using electric mixer, do not over-whip. Mix at slow speed.

COCOA-GRAHAM CRACKER CRUST

2 ⅓ cups graham cracker crumbs
¾ cup melted butter
⅓ cup superfine granulated sugar
⅔ cup sifted cocoa powder

Mix together crumbs, butter, sugar and cocoa until well incorporated. Press firmly into 9-inch pie plate to make solid bottom crust. Freeze until ready to use.

CHOCOLATE SAUCE

½ cup sugar
⅓ cup water
1 tablespoon corn syrup
2 ¼ ounces sweet chocolate, grated
¼ cup whipping cream

Combine sugar, water, corn syrup and chocolate in saucepan. Bring to boil. Remove immediately from heat and stir until smooth. In separate saucepan, bring cream to boil. Stir into chocolate mixture until smooth. Makes 1½ cups.

Sheraton Coconut Beach Hotel's Sand Pie

Sand pie as served at the Sheraton Coconut Beach Hotel in Hawaii is a great idea for holiday entertaining when you are looking for a do-ahead dessert.

2 pints plus ½ cup chocolate ice cream
Macadamia Nut Crust
2 pints vanilla ice cream
2 tablespoons hot fudge sauce
1 tablespoon coffee flavor liqueur
2 pints coffee ice cream
1 cup whipping cream
2 tablespoons sugar
½ teaspoon vanilla
½ cup coarsely chopped macadamia nuts

Spread 2 pints chocolate ice cream ¾ thick in bottom of cold Macadamia Nut Crust. Freeze. Top with ¾-inch-thick layer vanilla ice cream. Combine hot fudge sauce, coffee flavor liqueur and remaining ½ cup chocolate ice cream to make runny syrup. Lightly swirl mixture into vanilla layer. Freeze.

Spread layer of coffee ice cream ¾ inch thick on top of vanilla layer. Freeze. Beat whipping cream with sugar and vanilla until stiff. Top cake with sweetened whipped cream. Sprinkle with nuts. Freeze or serve. Makes 1 (9-inch) ice cream cake.

MACADAMIA NUT CRUST

3 ½ to 4 cups macadamia nut bits, chopped
½ cup flour
¼ cup brown sugar, packed
½ cup butter, melted

Combine nuts, flour, brown sugar and butter and mix well. Press firmly in bottom and sides of 9-inch springform pan. Bake at 325 degrees 15 minutes. Cool, then freeze.

PERSIMMON ICE CREAM PIE

This frozen pie comes out on holidays.

1/4 cup butter or margarine, melted
2 cups shredded coconut
1 quart vanilla ice cream
1 cup persimmon puree
1/2 cup sugar
1/4 teaspoon salt
1/4 teaspoon nutmeg
1/4 teaspoon cinnamon or ginger

Combine butter and coconut. Press evenly into 8 to 9-ich pie pan. Bake at 300 degrees 30 to 35 minutes, or until golden brown.

Soften ice cream. Combine persimmon puree, sugar, salt, nutmeg and cinnamon or ginger. Fold into ice cream. Turn into cooled pie shell. Freeze until firm, about 4 hours.

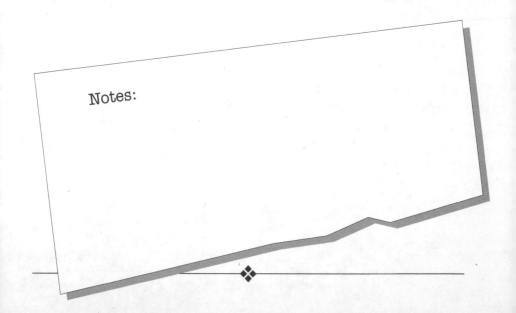

Notes:

PIER 4 ICE CREAM PIE

Owner Anthony Athanas of Anthony's Pier 4 in Boston sent us this recipe in 1975.

1 quart vanilla ice cream
1 (9-inch) graham cracker pie shell
Whipped cream
Hot Lemon Sauce

Soften ice cream and spread evenly in pie crust. Place in freezer until ready to serve.

To serve, slice pie into sixths. Pipe or spoon whipped cream around edge of pie and spoon Hot Lemon Sauce over center of pie. Makes about 6 servings.

HOT LEMON SAUCE

1 lemon
1 ¼ cups plus 5 tablespoons water
¾ cup sugar
2 tablespoons lemon juice concentrate
1 egg yolk
2 ½ tablespoons cornstarch

Grate zest and squeeze juice from lemon. Combine zest and juice with 1¼ cups water and sugar in top of double boiler over simmering water. Dissolve lemon juice concentrate in 5 tablespoons water and add to double boiler.

Beat egg yolk with 2½ tablespoons water and cornstarch, blending well. Bring lemon liquid to boil, then whisk in egg mixture. Simmer and stir until sauce thickens. Makes about 1 cup sauce.

❖

FRUIT DESSERTS

T hroughout "Culinary SOS" history, the most appealing fruit desserts have been the old-fashioned kind. *Rumtopf*, a fruit melange made up of seasonal fruit as the year progresses, is an ever-ready dessert for any impromptu occasion. Peaches are favored in almost any form, from *Peaches Melba*, served with ice cream, to Peach Ping, a form of a "crisp." *Bananas Foster*, a New Orleans restaurant favorite since the turn-of-the-century, and *Frozen Fruit Salad*, a product of the Industrial Revolution when refrigerators and freezer compartments came on the scene, are also popular to this day. Cobblers also have had wide appeal, and we've offered a recipe in which any fruit may be used. *Tarte Tatin* was introduced with the influx of modern French chefs to the United States in the early 1980s. It so happens that the recipe for the Tarte Tatin is from a popular bouillabaisse restaurant on the French Riviera, whose chef happily shared the recipe when we were visiting.

Dear S.O.S.:
I loved the strawberries flambé at Caesars Palace in Las Vegas and now can't wait to try it at home. Do you think Caesars will part with their recipe?
— Ruby

Dear Ruby:
We, too, loved the fancy table-side preparation of this wonderfully refreshing fruit dessert.

APPLE

APPLE COBBLER

This homey dessert can be served warm with ice cream or whipping cream (or both) on the side. You can substitute summer fruit, such as peaches, plums and apricots, in equal amounts.

> *7 cups sliced apples*
> *¾ cup sugar*
> *¼ teaspoon nutmeg*
> *⅛ teaspoon salt*
> *1 tablespoon lemon juice*
> *½ teaspoon grated lemon zest*
> *¼ teaspoon cinnamon*
> *2 tablespoons butter or margarine*
> *Prepared pastry for 1-crust pie*

Place apple slices in baking pan or casserole. Sprinkle with sugar, nutmeg, salt, lemon juice, lemon zest and cinnamon and dot with butter.

Roll out pastry to fit like lid over apple mixture. Place over apples and pierce crust with fork tines or cut slits in several places. Bake at 350 degrees 50 to 60 minutes. Makes 8 servings.

❖

APPLE PAN DOWDY

Pan dowdys are usually made in a skillet with biscuit crust dropped onto the fruit by spoonfuls like dumplings.

2 pounds tart green cooking apples, peeled, cored and sliced
1 tablespoon lemon juice
1/2 cup sugar
1 1/4 teaspoons ground cinnamon
1/2 teaspoon ground nutmeg
1/2 cup butter, cold and cut into 8 pieces
1/3 cup biscuit mix
1/8 teaspoon ginger
1/4 cup milk
Ice cream or whipped cream, optional

Toss apples in bowl with lemon juice. Put in large skillet with sugar, 1 teaspoon cinnamon and nutmeg and heat until bubbly. Stir in butter until melted.

Combine biscuit mix, remaining 1/4 teaspoon cinnamon, ginger and milk in separate bowl. Mix well with fork.

Drop batter by spoonfuls onto boiling apple mixture. Cook over low heat 10 minutes, uncovered, then cover and cook 10 minutes longer. Serve warm with ice cream or whipped cream. Makes 6 servings.

TARTE TATIN A LA NOUNOU

French chefs in Los Angeles introduced this spectacular upside-down apple cake cooked in caramel sauce. This version is from Nounou, a restaurant on the French Riviera.

1 cup butter
2 cups sugar
8 to 12 small Red Delicious apples
1 sheet frozen puff pastry
Vanilla ice cream

Place butter and sugar in heavy-gauge pan 2½ inches deep and 8 inches in diameter. Peel and core apples. Arrange apples snugly upright around edge of pan and in center over sugar mixture. Add more apples, if necessary, to keep pan snugly fitted with apples.

Place over low to medium heat and simmer 1 to 1½ hours or until sugar-butter syrup is golden caramel color. As apples cook, fit bits of apple in gaps where apples have shrunk.

Roll pastry sheet out onto floured board and form 9-inch circle. It should be very thin. Pierce with tines of fork and place over apples. Bake at 375 degrees 20 minutes or until crust is golden. Invert on platter, being careful sides do not fall away. With spatula or broad knife, smooth surface of apples and serve warm topped with small scoops of vanilla ice cream. Makes about 8 servings.

Note: In place of puff pastry use 6 sheets of filo dough. Stack, cut into 9-inch circle and brush each sheet with butter. Stack again and place over tart to bake as directed.

❖

BANANA

BANANAS FOSTER

This recipe for Bananas Foster is from Brennan's in New Orleans, but there are many versions of this extraordinarily simple, yet glamorous dessert. Be cautious when flaming the dish.

> *1 tablespoon butter*
> *¾ cup brown sugar, packed*
> *Dash ground cinnamon*
> *2 tablespoons banana liqueur*
> *6 bananas, halved lengthwise and crosswise*
> *¼ cup rum*
> *6 scoops vanilla ice cream*

Melt butter in chafing dish over alcohol burner. Add brown sugar, cinnamon and banana liqueur and stir to mix. Heat few minutes. Place halved bananas in sauce. Saute lightly until tender and lightly browned. Add rum and allow to heat well.

Ignite and allow sauce to flame until flames die out, tipping pan in circular motion to prolong flaming. Serve over vanilla ice cream, placing 4 banana pieces over each ice cream scoop, then spooning hot sauce over top. Makes 6 servings.

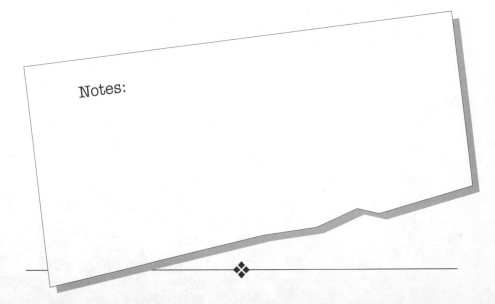

Notes:

CAESARS BANANAS AND STRAWBERRIES FLAMBÉ

Readers discovered this dessert at the Sunday buffet at Caesars Palace in Las Vegas.

1 tablespoon butter
2 bananas, quartered
Juice of ½ lemon
2 pints strawberries, hulled and halved or sliced
1 tablespoon sugar
½ cup orange juice
¼ cup Cognac
6 scoops vanilla ice cream (about 1 pint), optional

Melt butter in crepe pan over flame or brazier. Add banana quarters and sprinkle with lemon juice. Saute until bananas are glazed, but not mushy.

Add strawberries, sugar and orange juice. Cook over high heat until orange juice is almost absorbed.

Heat Cognac in small saucepan until warm. Ignite. *Warning:* Be careful to keep loose clothing, hair, face and hands away from the flames. After flame subsides, pour sauce over strawberry-banana mixture. Serve with scoop of ice cream. Makes 6 to 8 servings.

PEACH

PEACH PING

Just right for peach season.

> *10 to 12 large peaches*
> *½ cup butter or margarine*
> *1½ cups brown sugar, packed*
> *2 teaspoons grated lemon zest*
> *2 eggs*
> *2 cups granulated sugar*
> *½ cup boiling water*
> *2 teaspoons vanilla*
> *2 cups sifted flour*
> *1 teaspoon baking powder*
> *Dash salt*
> *Ice cream or whipped cream, optional*

Peel peaches, cut into quarters and arrange in 13 x 9-inch baking pan. Dot with butter, then sprinkle with brown sugar and lemon zest.

Beat eggs until light-colored. Gradually add granulated sugar and beat thoroughly. Stir in boiling water and vanilla.

Sift together flour, baking powder and salt. Add to egg mixture and blend well. Pour batter over peaches. Bake at 375 degrees 55 to 60 minutes or until crust is lightly browned and stiff when touched. Serve warm with ice cream or whipped cream. Makes 10 to 12 servings.

PEACHES MELBA

It's always a pleasure to print this classic recipe named after Nellie Melba, a turn-of-the-century Australian diva whose voice inspired a chef to create the dessert of ice cream and peaches.

1 (1-pound, 13-ounce) can peach halves
1 teaspoon vanilla
1/8 teaspoon ground nutmeg
1 cup raspberry jam
1/4 cup Port
1 quart vanilla ice cream
Toasted slivered almonds

Turn peaches into bowl and stir in vanilla and nutmeg. Let stand at room temperature 20 minutes to blend flavors, then chill thoroughly.

Beat together jam and Port until smooth. Drain peach halves and place cut side up in individual dessert dishes. Place scoop of ice cream in each peach half. Top with jam mixture and sprinkle with almonds. Makes 6 to 7 servings.

OTHER

Brandied Figs

Prepare them now for holiday gifts and parties later on in the year.

2 ½ cups brandy
5 pounds firm figs
5 cups sugar
2 ½ cups water

Pour brandy into jar and place in hot water to heat. Carefully wash figs and, if tough-skinned, peel. Pierce each fig in 2 or 3 places with large needle to prevent collapsing.

Combine sugar and water and cook until sugar dissolves. Add figs and boil gently 6 to 10 minutes or until tender.

Remove figs from syrup with slotted spoon and place in hot, sterilized pint jars set in hot water. Boil syrup rapidly 5 to 8 minutes to thicken.

Pour ½ cup hot brandy over figs in each jar and fill to within ⅛ inch of top with boiling hot syrup. Seal jars at once. Makes about 5 pints.

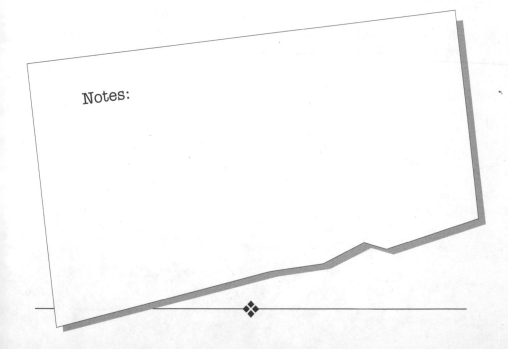

Notes:

FRUIT PIZZA

Fruit Pizza made with a cookie-crust base can be varied according to the fruit in season.

1 (18-ounce) package refrigerated sugar cookie dough
1 (8-ounce) package cream cheese, softened
⅓ cup sugar
½ teaspoon vanilla
2 peaches, peeled and sliced
½ cup blueberries
½ cup strawberry halves
½ cup seedless green grape halves
½ cup orange marmalade
2 tablespoons water

Slice cookie dough into ⅛-inch slices. Arrange slices, overlapping slightly, on 14-inch pizza pan. Bake at 375 degrees 12 minutes or until crust is light golden brown. Cool on wire rack.

Meanwhile, beat cream cheese with sugar and vanilla. Spread over cooled crust. Arrange peaches, blueberries, strawberries and grapes over cooled crust. Mix marmalade with water in small saucepan. Heat until marmalade liquefies. Brush over fruit. Makes 6 servings.

❖

STRAWBERRIES ROMANOFF

This dessert is said to have been served at Romanoff's when it was a celebrity hangout during Hollywood's Golden Era in Los Angeles.

¼ cup strawberry liqueur
¼ cup orange liqueur
2 tablespoons Cognac
Brown sugar, optional
Juice 1 lemon
2 baskets strawberries
3 pints French vanilla ice cream
1 cup whipping cream, whipped

In bowl, combine strawberry liqueur, orange liqueur, Cognac, up to 2 tablespoons brown sugar, depending on sweetness of berries, and lemon juice.

Rinse strawberries, reserving 8 for garnish. Hull and halve remaining strawberries. Marinate halved strawberries in liqueur mixture about 15 minutes.

In large bowl, soften 2 pints vanilla ice cream, then fold in whipped cream. Fold in marinated strawberry mixture.

Place small scoop of remaining ice cream in 8 large stemmed glasses. Fill glasses with mixture, then garnish each with reserved whole strawberry. Sprinkle with additional brown sugar to taste, if desired. Serve at once. Makes 8 servings.

Rumtopf

Jars of rumtopf, the German name for fruit preserved in brandy or rum, can be replenished with seasonal fruit throughout the year to serve over ice cream, pound cake or alone.

1 (750-milliliter) bottle rum, bourbon or brandy
Peel of 1 orange, cut in spiral
1 tablespoon whole cloves
1 stick cinnamon
1 teaspoon whole allspice
1 pound cherries, pitted
8 cups sugar
1 pound peaches, peeled and pitted
1 pound apricots, peeled and pitted
1 pound plums, pitted
1 pound seedless grapes
1 pint strawberries, hulled
1 pint raspberries
1 pound pineapple, peeled, cored and cut in slices

Scald 6-quart stone crock or glass jar with boiling water and dry. Pour liquor into crock and add orange peel, cloves, cinnamon stick and allspice. Add cherries and 1 cup sugar. Stir gently, cover crock with foil and set aside in cool spot or refrigerate.

Continue adding layers of fruit and sugar as fruits come in season. Add at intervals of not less than 1 week. For each pound or pint of fruit added, add 1 cup sugar. Stir gently each time fruit and sugar are added.

Keep crock covered with foil, held in place with small plate if necessary. Add more liquor if fruit absorbs initial amount. After sufficient fruit is added, put crock in cool, dark place to ripen 2 to 3 months or as long as possible.

If only small amount of rumtopf mixture is used at time, 1 pound fruit and 1 cup sugar may be added to replenish the supply. Fruit must be ripe, blemish-free and well-cleaned.

After all fruit has been added and stirred, the mixture can be spooned into hot sterilized jars and processed in boiling-water bath 15 minutes if longer storage is desired. Serve as sauce over pudding or ice cream or as topping for pound cake. Makes about 1 gallon.

❖

APPLE-CRANBERRY CRISP

This crisp or "buckle" is popular in New England.

1 pound apples, peeled, cored and cut in wedges
1 cup cranberries
¼ cup coarsely chopped walnuts or pecans
⅓ to ½ cup granulated sugar
¼ cup brown sugar, packed
¼ cup oats
1 tablespoon flour
⅛ teaspoon ground cinnamon
⅛ teaspoon ground nutmeg
1½ tablespoons butter, slightly softened
Vanilla ice cream or whipping cream, optional

Mix apple wedges, cranberries and nuts in 8-inch-square baking dish. Sprinkle with granulated sugar.

In another bowl, combine brown sugar, oats, flour, cinnamon, nutmeg and butter. Mix with fingers until crumbly. Sprinkle topping evenly over apples.

Bake at 350 degrees 25 to 35 minutes or until apples are tender and top is crisp. Let cool slightly before serving. Serve with ice cream. Makes 4 servings.

❖

CONFECTIONS

There is nothing sweeter in this dessert book than what's featured in this chapter — truffles and fudges of all types, including *Paddy's Potatoes*, a peanut-butter mixture shaped like potatoes for St. Patrick's Day festivities, the ever-popular *Can't Fail Fudge* and *Vanilla Fudge*. Also here are such popcorn-and-nut favorites as *Honey Crackle* and *Peanut Clusters*. *Sea Foam*, *Honeycomb* and *Sesame Honey Balls* round out the selection.

Dear S.O.S.:
    St. Patrick's Day is coming up and I'd love the recipe for the peanut butter confections shaped like small potatoes. Any chance of a recipe?
    – Darlene

Dear Darlene:
    Leprechauns dug out the recipe for Paddy's Potatoes.

FRUIT

CANDIED CITRUS FRUIT PEEL

Readers love to make their own Candied Citrus Fruit Peel for holiday baking.

3 large oranges with thick shiny skin
1 grapefruit, preferably pink
2 large limes
2 lemons
Sugar

With knife, make incisions through skin of each orange, grapefruit, lime and lemon to separate into 6 sections. Separate skins from fruit. Place peel in pot and cover with cold water. Use enough water so peels are well covered. Bring to strong boil and let boil about 30 seconds. Pour into colander and rinse with cold water.

Rinse pot, add peel with water to cover and repeat boiling and rinsing procedure. Return peel to clean pot again and add 8 cups water and 1½ cups sugar. Bring to boil and simmer gently, uncovered, about 1½ hours. Peel should almost be transparent, and there should just be enough thick syrup to coat them.

Transfer peels to tray covered with sugar. Roll peel in sugar to coat. Arrange on another tray and let cool, dry and harden overnight. Makes 4 dozen.

CANDIED FIGS

Making Candied Figs is a bit of business, but well worth it if you have food gifts in mind for the holiday season.

4 ½ cups sugar plus extra for coating
5 pounds figs, preferably white or Kadota
¼ cup baking soda

Stir sugar and 2 cups water in large saucepan until sugar is dissolved. Bring to boil over high heat.

Place figs in another saucepan and sprinkle with baking soda. Cover with boiling water and let stand 10 minutes. Drain and rinse figs. Let stand 10 minutes in cold water and drain again.

Drop figs into boiling syrup. Reduce heat to simmer and cook figs, uncovered, 2 hours. Cover and simmer 30 minutes longer. Let stand in syrup overnight.

Spread figs 1 layer deep on trays or baking sheets lined with cheesecloth. Cover with another layer of cheesecloth, fastening top and bottom layers of cheesecloth with clothespins. Let dry in sun 4 to 5 days, turning each day. (Bring trays in at night.) When figs are dry but not hard, press flat. Roll in sugar and store in airtight containers with wax paper between layers. Makes about 5 pounds.

CHOCOLATE-DIPPED STRAWBERRIES

Chocolate-covered strawberries are great for bridal showers, weddings or other special occasions.

1 (12-ounce) package semisweet chocolate pieces
6 tablespoons butter
½ teaspoon vanilla
Strawberries

Melt chocolate pieces in top of double boiler. Add butter and vanilla. Dip strawberries in chocolate, swirling to coat only. Place on wax paper and set in cool dry place. Makes 6 to 12 dipped strawberries (depending on size).

Note: Cherries or other fruit may be substituted for strawberries.

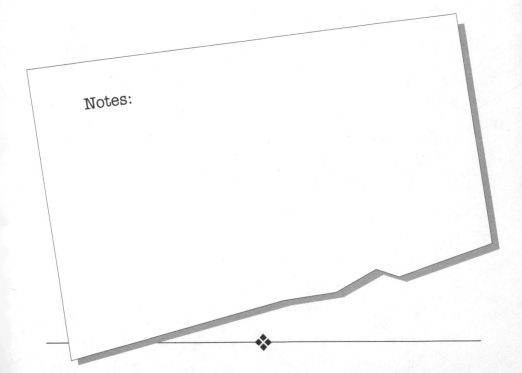

Notes:

GELATIN APPLE CANDY

Here is a version of the commercial gelatin candy that brings frequent reader requests.

8 medium apples
½ cup cold water
2 cups brown sugar, packed
2 envelopes unflavored gelatin
1 cup chopped walnuts
1 tablespoon lemon juice
½ cup powdered sugar
1 tablespoon cornstarch

Core and peel apples. Cut into small pieces. Add ¼ cup cold water. Cook until tender, then put through food mill or sieve. Add brown sugar. Cook and stir over low heat until thick, about 30 minutes.

Soften gelatin in remaining ¼ cup cold water, then add to hot apple mixture. Stir until dissolved. Chill until slightly thickened. Stir in walnuts and lemon juice. Pour into 8- or 9-inch square pan to depth of about ½ inch. Chill thoroughly. Cut into ¾ to 1-inch squares. Combine powdered sugar and cornstarch. Dredge squares in sugar mixture. Makes 6 to 7 dozen squares.

PARISIAN SWEETS

These are easy to make for last-minute gifts or the holiday candy dish.

1 pound dried pitted dates or figs
Powdered sugar
1 cup chopped flaked coconut
Maraschino or candied cherries, optional

Put dates or figs through food chopper, using fine blade. Place ground fruit on board dusted heavily with powdered sugar and knead until well blended and mixture clings together. Dust hands with powdered sugar and shape candy into $3\frac{1}{2}$ x $\frac{1}{2}$-inch fingers. Roll in coconut and press 1 cherry half into each roll. Makes about 2 pounds.

PEACH LEATHER

Do take advantage of the lower prices of summer fruit to make Peach Leather.

10 large fully ripe peaches, nectarines, plums or apricots
1 cup sugar

Peel and slice peaches to measure 10 cups. Place fruit in large saucepan. Add sugar and bring mixture to boil, stirring until sugar is dissolved. Pour mixture into blender container and purée. Cool to lukewarm.

Meanwhile, prepare smooth, level drying surface in full sunlight. Cover baking sheets, jelly-roll pans or other flat surfaces with plastic wrap. Pour peach purée onto prepared surface, spread to ⅛-inch thickness and let dry in sunlight. Protect from insects.

Drying may take 20 to 24 hours. Bring inside at end of day and finish drying second day. Or set sheets of fruit in baking pans in oven at 150 degrees and leave door open. Fruit is dry when purée can be peeled off plastic easily.

For storing, roll up leather with plastic wrap. Wrap in more plastic wrap and seal tightly. Leather will keep at room temperature about 1 month; in refrigerator 4 months; in freezer 1 year. Tear or cut into strips to eat. Makes 3 (15 x 10-inch) sheets.

FUDGE

CAN'T FAIL FUDGE

Can't Fail Fudge hasn't failed readers with a passion for chocolate yet.

4 cups miniature marshmallows
⅔ cup evaporated milk
¼ cup butter or margarine
1 ½ cups sugar
¼ teaspoon salt
1 (12-ounce) package semisweet chocolate pieces
1 teaspoon vanilla
½ cup chopped walnuts

Combine marshmallows, milk, butter, sugar and salt in saucepan. Cook and stir until mixture comes to full boil. Boil 5 minutes over medium heat, stirring constantly.

Remove from heat and add chocolate pieces, beating until melted. Fold in vanilla and nuts. Pour into greased 9-inch-square pan. Chill until firm. Makes 2½ pounds.

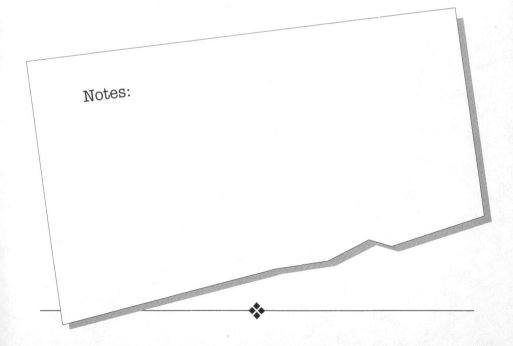

Notes:

MASHED POTATO FUDGE

This delicious fudge is made with mashed potatoes, chocolate and coconut.

¼ cup hot mashed potatoes
1 teaspoon butter or margarine
2 ½ cups sifted powdered sugar
½ teaspoon vanilla
Dash salt
1 ⅓ cups shredded coconut
2 squares unsweetened chocolate, melted

Mix potatoes and butter in bowl. Add sugar gradually and beat until well blended. Add vanilla, salt and coconut. Pack in greased 8 x 4-inch loaf pan. Spread chocolate over top. Chill until chocolate is firm. Cut in squares. Makes 1¼ pounds.

Note: If desired, 4 squares candy-making chocolate, melted, may be substituted for unsweetened chocolate in recipe.

Notes:

PADDY'S POTATOES

No-cook peanut-butter candies, shaped and sprinkled with cocoa and nuts to resemble potatoes, are a safe and fun-filled project for children of all ages.

> *5 tablespoons butter or margarine, melted*
> *1 cup peanut butter*
> *¼ teaspoon salt*
> *½ teaspoon vanilla*
> *Powdered sugar*
> *½ teaspoon ground cinnamon*
> *2 teaspoons cocoa powder*
> *2 teaspoons chopped nuts*

Mix butter and peanut butter until blended. Add salt and vanilla. Gradually add 1½ cups powdered sugar until mixture can be molded into potato-like shapes.

In separate bowl, combine 1 tablespoon powdered sugar, cinnamon, cocoa and nuts. Roll balls in mixture. Store in cold place until candy hardens. Makes about 3 dozen.

❖

PEANUT BUTTER-CHOCOLATE FUDGE

A peanut butter-chocolate fudge recipe that contains Reese's peanut butter chips as well as chocolate chips is a great holiday favorite.

¾ cup evaporated milk
¼ cup butter
2¼ cups sugar
1 (7-ounce) jar marshmallow cream
6 ounces peanut butter-flavor pieces
6 ounces semisweet chocolate pieces
1 teaspoon vanilla extract
1 cup broken walnuts

Combine evaporated milk, butter, sugar and marshmallow cream in heavy 3-quart saucepan. Cook over medium heat, stirring constantly, until mixture begins to boil. Continue cooking and stirring 5 minutes.

Remove from heat and add peanut butter pieces, chocolate pieces and vanilla, stirring until chips melt. Add walnuts. Pour into buttered 9-inch-square pan. Cool and cut into 1-inch squares. Makes 64 squares.

VANILLA FUDGE

This is like the vanilla fudge with almonds sold commercially.

2 cups evaporated milk
6 cups sugar
1 teaspoon salt
6 tablespoons butter or margarine
1 ½ teaspoons vanilla
1 cup marshmallow cream
¾ cup chopped or whole almonds
1 cup tiny chocolate pieces

Combine milk, sugar, salt and butter in 4-quart saucepan. Mix thoroughly. Cook over medium heat, stirring constantly, to 236 degrees on candy thermometer or until candy forms soft ball when dropped into cold water. Full rolling boil should be maintained throughout. Remove from heat.

Cool at room temperature without stirring until lukewarm. Blend in vanilla. Work in marshmallow cream and nuts, stirring until candy loses its gloss. Remove from heat and stir in chocolate pieces. Quickly spread in greased 12 x 7-inch pan. Makes about 5 pounds, about 5 dozen pieces.

NUTS

HONEYED NUTS

Readers like preparing these for Christmas.

1 ½ cups sugar
¼ teaspoon salt
¼ cup honey
½ cup water
½ teaspoon vanilla
3 cups walnut halves, pecan halves or other nuts

Combine sugar, salt, honey and water in saucepan. Cook, uncovered, to 242 degrees on candy thermometer or to firm soft ball stage. Remove from heat, add vanilla and nuts and stir until creamy. Turn out onto wax paper and separate nuts with two forks as they cool. Makes about 1 quart.

SUGARED AND SPICED NUTS

Sugared nuts, like the ones you can buy at great expense in stores, are easy to make at home.

1 egg white
1 tablespoon water
1 pound pecan or walnut halves, or half pound of each
2/3 cup superfine sugar
1 teaspoon salt
2 teaspoons ground cinnamon
3/4 teaspoon ground ginger
3/4 teaspoon ground allspice
1/2 teaspoon ground coriander

Whisk egg white and water until foamy. Stir in nuts and mix well. Pour into sieve and drain 3 minutes.

Combine sugar, salt, cinnamon, ginger, allspice and coriander in paper bag. Gather bag at neck and shake to mix spices. Add drained nuts and shake bag vigorously to coat with sugar and spices.

Spread nuts on 2 baking sheets, making sure nuts do not touch. Arrange 1 shelf in lower third and 1 in upper third of oven. Bake at 250 degrees 15 minutes, then stir. Spread out again. Lower oven temperature to 225 degrees and continue to bake, stirring occasionally, until well dried and crisp, about 1¼ hours longer. (At midpoint, switch shelf positions of 2 pans.) Turn off oven and let nuts cool with oven door open. Store completely cooled nuts in airtight containers. Makes about 1½ pounds.

OTHER

CHOCOLATE-COVERED SEA FOAM

Readers love a recipe for sea foam covered with chocolate.

3 cups brown sugar
1 cup water
1 tablespoon vinegar
2 egg whites
⅛ teaspoon salt
1 teaspoon vanilla
½ pound bittersweet, semisweet or milk chocolate

Mix sugar, water and vinegar in saucepan and place over low heat. Stir until sugar is dissolved. Cook mixture quickly to soft ball stage, 238 degrees on candy thermometer.

Beat egg whites and salt in bowl until whites are stiff. Pour syrup over egg whites in thin stream, beating constantly. Place bowl over, but not in, boiling water and beat until candy is thick and creamy. Add vanilla.

Pour candy onto greased platter and cut into squares while hot. Cool. Melt chocolate in top of double boiler over simmering water. Remove chocolate from heat. Pierce 1 square of sea foam with metal skewer and dip or roll in melted chocolate until completely coated with chocolate, tilting pan if necessary. Continue to coat remaining squares of sea foam. Makes about 1 pound.

CHOCOLATE TRUFFLES

We hope these truffles exceed your expectations.

7 ounces semisweet or bittersweet chocolate
¼ cup whipping cream
½ cup unsalted butter, cut up
2 to 3 teaspoons Grand Marnier, amaretto, framboise, Cognac,
    brandy, creme de menthe or rum
1 cup Dutch process cocoa or 2 cups finely chopped walnuts, almonds,
    hazelnuts, pecans or pistachios

Coarsely chop chocolate. Place in top of double boiler and add whipping cream and butter. Heat over simmering water, stirring constantly until chocolate and butter melt and mixture becomes satiny smooth.

Remove top of double boiler from heat. Stir in liqueur. Cool slightly. Refrigerate 2 hours or until chocolate mixture is firm.

Working quickly, form mixture into 1-inch balls. (Balls may melt slightly on outside.) Drop into bowl of cocoa or chopped nuts, coating truffles on all sides. Place on wax paper.

Repeat procedure until all chocolate mixture is used. If mixture becomes too soft, return to refrigerator ½ hour or more. Truffles may be refrigerated 1 hour after making to firm further. Serve at room temperature. Makes 20 to 30 truffles.

ENGLISH TOFFEE

You can vary the nuts used in toffee.

½ pound butter
1 cup sugar
¼ pound (about 1 cup) whole blanched almonds
2 (1-ounce) squares semisweet chocolate, melted
½ cup or more finely chopped walnuts

Melt butter over medium heat. Add sugar and boil 5 minutes, stirring constantly. Stir in almonds. Boil 3 to 5 minutes longer or until golden brown, stirring. Pour into ungreased 9-inch-square pan. Cool. Remove from pan and spread melted chocolate over top. Sprinkle with walnuts. When chocolate is set, break into pieces. Makes 1 pound.

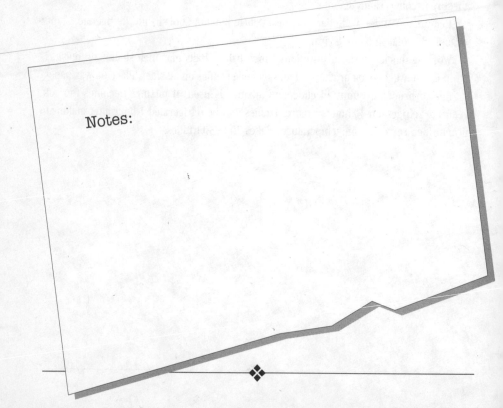

Notes:

HONEY CRACKLE

This popcorn confection comes under the name of caramel nut corn or Honey Crackle.

3 quarts freshly popped corn
1 cup blanched slivered almonds
½ cup butter or margarine
1 cup brown sugar, packed
¼ cup honey
1 teaspoon vanilla

Turn popped corn into large, shallow roasting pan. Sprinkle almonds over corn.

Melt butter in 1-quart saucepan. Stir in sugar and honey. Cook, stirring, over medium heat until mixture comes to boil. Simmer without stirring 5 minutes.

Remove from heat and stir in vanilla. Pour mixture over popped corn and almonds and stir until well mixed. Bake at 250 degrees, stirring every 15 minutes, 1 hour. Cool completely. Break apart and store in tightly covered container. Makes about 3 quarts.

MICROWAVE HONEYCOMB

This "honeycomb" candy recipe is prepared in a microwave. If you're using a saucepan instead, heat the sugar-corn syrup mixture to 300 degrees (the hard ball stage on a candy thermometer), then quickly stir in the baking soda.

1 cup sugar
1 cup dark corn syrup
1 tablespoon white vinegar
1 tablespoon baking soda

Combine sugar, corn syrup and vinegar in 2-quart microwaveable bowl and cook on high (600 to 700 watts) 3 minutes. Stir through several times. Continue cooking on high until mixture has thickened and candy thermometer registers 300 degrees, or until small amount dropped into cold water separates into hard and brittle threads, 7 to 10 minutes.

Quickly stir in baking soda (mixture will foam), blending thoroughly. Do not over-stir. Pour into 8-inch-square baking dish lined with generously greased foil, tilting to cover bottom evenly. Cool at room temperature until firm, about 1 hour. Do not refrigerate. Break honeycomb into pieces and place on wax paper. Cool at room temperature. Makes about 1 pound.

SESAME HONEY BALLS

There is hardly any candy easier to make than these sesame balls made in a blender.

1 cup sesame seeds
2 tablespoons honey
¼ teaspoon vanilla

Place seeds in blender container and blend until consistency of peanut butter. Add honey and vanilla and blend until smooth. Shape into ½- to ¾-inch balls. Serve in tiny paper cup liners. Makes about 8 balls.

PEANUT CLUSTERS

These Peanut Clusters call for butterscotch and chocolate pieces.

1 (6-ounce) package chocolate pieces
1 (12 ounce) package butterscotch pieces
1 (12-ounce) package salted Spanish peanuts

Combine chocolate and butterscotch pieces in heavy 2-quart saucepan. Cook on medium heat until melted. Stir once during melting. Stir in peanuts. Drop by teaspoons onto wax paper. Let set until firm. Store airtight. Makes 3½ to 4 dozen.

PRESERVES

R eaders' preferences for preserves seem to reflect the times. Today's convenience- and health-minded readers often request no-cook or sugar-free jam. These share the chapter with such old-fashioned favorites as *Preserved Kumquats* and *Pineapple Jam*.

Dear S.O.S.:
 I have an overload of kumquats from my tree. Do you have a recipe for preserves?
 —Janice

Dear Janice:
 Kumquat preserves has been a seasonal favorite and one especially suited to turning into holiday gifts.

FRESH FIG JAM

An easy-to-make fresh fig jam relies on strawberry gelatin.

3 cups peeled, mashed figs (about 20)
1 (6-ounce) package strawberry gelatin
3 cups sugar

Thoroughly mix figs, gelatin and sugar in large kettle. Bring to boil over medium heat and boil 3 minutes, stirring occasionally. Pour quickly into sterilized glasses and cover at once with ⅛-inch hot paraffin. Makes enough for about 6 medium glasses.

PINEAPPLE JAM

The high cost of pineapple jam often prompts readers to request a home recipe.

1 medium pineapple, peeled, cored and cut into chunks
¼ cup lemon juice
7 cups sugar
1 (6-ounce) pouch liquid pectin

Grind pineapple chunks in blender or food processor. In strainer, drain about 2 hours to extract ¾ cup pineapple juice. In saucepan, combine pulp (about 2½ to 3 cups), ¾ cup pineapple juice, lemon juice and sugar. Bring to full rolling boil and boil hard 1 minute, stirring constantly.

Remove from heat and stir in pectin. Stir and skim 5 minutes to prevent fruit from floating. Pour into hot sterilized glasses, leaving ⅛-inch head space. Wipe sealing edge of jars. Adjust lids and sterilize in boiling water bath 5 minutes. Cool. Test seals and store. Makes 9 (6-ounce) glasses.

Notes:

PINK GRAPEFRUIT MARMALADE

Long-time readers might remember the still-popular recipe for pink grapefruit marmalade.

⅔ cup thinly sliced grapefruit or lemon peel
1 ⅓ cups chopped pink or white grapefruit or lemon pulp
*   (about 1 grapefruit or 2 ½ large lemons)*
Sugar

Place peel in saucepan and add enough water to cover. Bring to boil and boil 10 minutes. Drain. Repeat 2 or 3 times. Add chopped pulp and 4 cups water to drained peel, cover and let stand 12 to 18 hours in cool place.

After soaking, cook grapefruit mixture rapidly until peel is tender, about 40 minutes. Measure fruit and liquid. Add 1 cup sugar for each cup fruit mixture.

Bring slowly to boil, stirring until sugar dissolves. Cook rapidly almost to jellying point, about 30 to 35 minutes. Stir occasionally to prevent sticking. Pour boiling hot into sterilized jars and seal. Makes about 3 half-pints.

PRESERVED KUMQUATS

Kumquat season often brings out the fans of this unique preserve because they make great holiday gifts wrapped in gingham cloth and ribbon.

1 pound kumquats
1 ½ teaspoons baking soda
2 cups sugar
1 ½ teaspoons whole cloves
4 broken cinnamon sticks

Rinse kumquats in warm water. Sprinkle with baking soda. In bowl, cover kumquats with boiling water. Let stand 10 minutes. Pour off hot water, then rinse 3 times in cold water.

Cut tiny cross in blossom end of each fruit. Place in cold water to cover. Bring to boil and boil 15 minutes. Drain, add fresh water and repeat boiling process until fruit is tender. Drain and set aside.

In pot, combine sugar, cloves and cinnamon sticks with 2 cups water and bring to boil. Boil 5 minutes. Add boiled kumquats and cook in syrup until fruit is transparent and syrup registers 222 degrees on candy thermometer.

Remove pan from heat. Let kumquats plump in syrup at room temperature overnight or longer. Drain kumquats, reserving syrup. Reheat syrup to boiling. Place kumquats in sterilized jars and strain hot syrup over fruit, filling jars to within ½ inch of top. Seal jars by processing in boiling-water bath 10 minutes. Makes 3 to 4 half-pints.

SUGAR-FREE PEACH JAM

Here's a peach jam recipe using gelatin instead of sugar to thicken the jam.

1 envelope unflavored gelatin
¼ cup cold water
1 ½ cups peeled, sliced peaches
1 teaspoon lemon juice
1 teaspoon granulated or few drops liquid noncaloric sweetener

Soften gelatin in cold water. Place peaches in saucepan, sprinkle with lemon juice and bring to boil. Add softened gelatin and blend well. Add sweetener to taste and remove from heat. Pour into 2 sterilized half-pint jars and seal immediately. Do not use paraffin. Let cool. Store in refrigerator until used. Makes about 1½ cups.

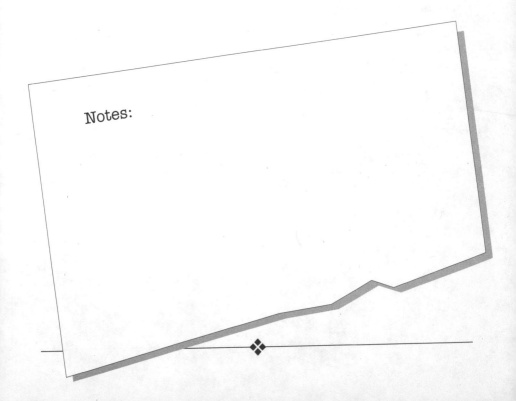

Notes:

KIWI JAM

This can be stored in the refrigerator to be eaten within a week or two, or frozen.

3 ½ cups well-mashed kiwi
¼ cup lemon juice
1 package powdered pectin
1 cup light corn syrup
4 ½ cups sugar

Mix kiwi pulp and lemon juice thoroughly in large saucepan. Sift in pectin, stirring vigorously. Add corn syrup and mix well.

Gradually stir in sugar, stirring until completely dissolved. Warming to 100 degrees on candy thermometer (no hotter) will help dissolve sugar. Jam is ready to eat when sugar is dissolved.

Spoon into sterilized glasses or containers with tight-fitting lids. Store in freezer for lengthy storage or refrigerator if to be eaten within a week or two. Makes 2 pints.

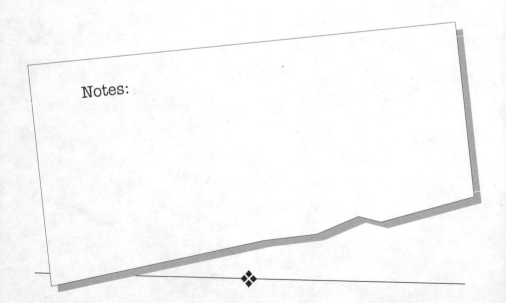

Notes:

CRANBERRY CHUTNEY

A favorite chutney for holiday meals and beyond.

1 pound fresh cranberries
2 cups sugar
1 cup water
1 cup orange juice
1 cup raisins, coarsely chopped
1 cup chopped walnuts
1 cup chopped celery
1 cup finely chopped tart apples (Granny Smith)
1 tablespoon grated orange zest
1 teaspoon ground ginger
3 tablespoons finely chopped candied ginger

Sort through and discard bruised cranberries. Rinse berries and drain. Combine berries with sugar and water in large saucepan. Place over medium heat and bring to boil, stirring occasionally. Simmer 15 minutes and remove from heat. Stir in orange juice, raisins, walnuts, celery, apples, orange zest, ground and candied ginger. Cool completely. Spoon chutney into sterilized storage jars and refrigerate. Makes about 7 cups.

Note: Prepare chutney at last 2 hours before serving and preferably 1 week or more in advance. Chutney will keep up to 3 weeks, if refrigerated.

BEVERAGES

Beverages are not actually desserts, but they are often so sweet and satisfying that they double as dessert. We have included several popular drinks, including a lemon whipped cream called *Syllabub*, which should suit dessert lovers. There's also a homemade Galliano-type liqueur that can be made and given as a gift.

Dear S.O.S.:
I hear that you have the recipe for former President Reagan's favorite eggnog.
— Charles

Dear Charles:
The recipe was sent from The White House during the president's term in office. It's been a favorite since.

Almost Like Orange Julius

The Orange Julius people understandably cannot divulge the trade secret of their juice-stand drink, but with the help of readers, we have developed several versions, including this one, which could almost fool you.

> *½ (6-ounce) can frozen orange juice concentrate*
> *½ cup milk*
> *½ cup water*
> *¼ cup sugar*
> *½ teaspoon vanilla*
> *5 to 6 ice cubes*

Combine orange juice concentrate, milk, water, sugar, vanilla and ice cubes in blender container. Cover and blend until smooth, about 30 seconds. Serve immediately. Makes about 2 servings.

BERRY LIQUEUR

A splash of berry-flavored liqueur can be added to champagne for a festive drink or punch.

> *4 cups blueberries or other berries*
> *3 cups vodka*
> *1 cup water*
> *$\frac{1}{2}$ teaspoon whole cloves*
> *$\frac{1}{2}$ teaspoon coriander seeds*
> *2 cups sugar*

Mash berries and place in large glass jar. Add vodka, water, cloves and coriander seeds. Cover container and let stand at room temperature 10 days. Strain mixture through fine sieve into another glass jar. Discard residue. Add sugar and stir until dissolved. Let stand at room temperature about 24 hours. Pour through fine-mesh strainer or cheesecloth. Place in bottle and cap. Makes 1 quart.

CAPPUCCINO SAN FRANCISCO

This is an easy San Francisco version of cappuccino made with instant chocolate drink mix and half and half. The brandy, of course, is optional.

> *2 cups hot strong coffee*
> *2 tablespoons instant chocolate drink mix*
> *2 cups half and half, scalded*
> *2 to 3 ounces brandy, optional*
> *Sugar*

Stir hot coffee into chocolate mix, blending well. Add hot half and half. Stir in brandy and sugar to taste. Makes 4 to 6 cups.

SUSAN'S GALLIANO-TYPE LIQUEUR

Many years ago, a reader sent us her version of a recipe for a Galliano-type liqueur with vodka and Strega, the anise flavoring characteristic of Galliano.

> *4 cups sugar*
> *2 cups water*
> *2 cups 100-proof vodka*
> *1 (¹/₂-ounce) bottle Strega extract*
> *Dash yellow food color*

Combine sugar and water; cook until syrupy. Cool. Add vodka, Strega and food color and mix well. Place in glass jar or bottle and let stand 30 days before using. Makes 2 (fifth) bottles.

Note: Strega extract is generally available at Italian import grocery stores.

HORCHATA DE ARROZ *(Ground Rice Drink)*

This refreshing Mexican beverage made from rice is a conversation piece at parties.

> *½ cup rice*
> *3 ½ cups water*
> *¼ teaspoon ground cinnamon, heaping*
> *½ teaspoon cornstarch, blended with small amount of*
> *   cold water*
> *¾ cup powdered sugar*

Combine rice and 2 cups water in saucepan. Bring to boil and boil about 7 minutes, until rice is tender, but not soft. Place rice in blender. Add remaining 1½ cups water and blend. Add cinnamon, cornstarch mixture and powdered sugar and blend again.

To serve, combine rice mixture with water in proportion of ⅔ cup rice mixture to 1 cup water. Stir and add more sugar, if desired. Serve over ice. Makes 3¾ cups rice mixture.

LEMON SYLLABUB

Keep this traditional "drink" in mind for a do-ahead holiday dessert.

> *2 lemons*
> *1 tablespoon medium Sherry*
> *2 tablespoons brandy*
> *2 tablespoons dry white wine, optional*
> *3 tablespoons sugar*
> *1 pint whipping cream*

Finely grate lemon peels and combine with juice of 1 lemon in small bowl. Add Sherry, brandy, wine and sugar and marinate overnight. Whip cream until soft peaks form. Fold into marinade. Pour into wine glasses and refrigerate 2 hours. Makes 6 to 8 servings.

President Reagan's Favorite Eggnog

A recipe from a former White House chef for President Ronald Reagan's favorite eggnog has become a holiday must for countless readers.

1 ½ cups sugar
1 tablespoon vanilla
6 eggs or equal amount commercial egg substitute
3 cups half and half
1 cup bourbon
1 cup brandy
1 cup rum
Freshly grated nutmeg

Place sugar, vanilla and eggs in blender. Blend until thoroughly mixed. Add half and half. Blend well.

Pour into serving bowl. Add bourbon, brandy and rum. Stir until well mixed. Dust top of each serving with nutmeg. Makes 12 servings, 2 quarts.

Note: See warning on the use of raw eggs, page 256.

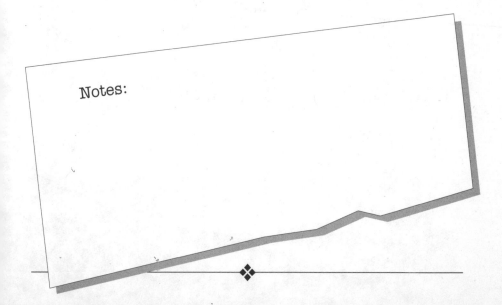

Notes:

❖

MISCELLANEOUS

S ome recipes enhance other desserts. There are sauces for ice cream and puddings, cake frostings, pastry crusts, plus a few extras to keep on hand for a rainy day.

Dear S.O.S.:
    I like hot fudge that remains thick after pouring. Do you have such a recipe?
    —Carole

Dear Carole:
    This hot fudge unfurls like a ribbon.

FROSTINGS

BAKERY-TYPE CREAMY FROSTING

Bakery-type creamy frostings are best for decorating cakes.

2 tablespoons flour
½ cup milk
½ cup sugar
¼ cup margarine
¼ cup shortening
Dash salt
½ cup powdered sugar
1 teaspoon vanilla

Mix flour with milk in small saucepan. Cook over low heat until thickened, stirring constantly. Cool. Cream sugar and margarine with shortening until fluffy. Add salt and cold flour-milk paste and beat until doubled. Beat in powdered sugar and vanilla. Makes about 1 cup.

HEIRLOOM BOILED FROSTING

The frosting keeps in the refrigerator for several days and can be reconstituted by being beaten again. Use a candy thermometer to assure proper syrup temperature.

2 cups sugar
½ cup light corn syrup
½ cup water
2 egg whites
1 ½ teaspoons vanilla

Combine sugar, corn syrup and water in saucepan. Place over moderate heat and stir until sugar is dissolved. Continue to boil to soft ball stage (239 degrees on candy thermometer on dry day or 242 degrees on rainy day).

Meanwhile beat egg whites in large bowl until stiff. Add syrup in thin stream, continuing to beat rapidly. Add vanilla and continue to beat until cold and stiff enough to hold shape.

Frosting can be kept in covered jar in refrigerator several days. When ready to use, beat in ½ teaspoon or so of boiling water to soften frosting. If frosting hardens at any stage, beating in boiling water will aid in keeping it spreadable. Makes enough to frost 3-layer cake.

❖

MARSHMALLOW FROSTING

A frosting made with marshmallows.

32 marshmallows
⅔ cup milk
¾ cup butter or margarine
1 teaspoon vanilla

Combine marshmallows and milk. Cook over low heat until marshmallows dissolve. Cool to room temperature, stirring to blend thoroughly.

Cream butter until light and fluffy at medium speed of electric mixer. Continue to beat, gradually adding marshmallow mixture. Add vanilla. Continue beating until mixture is stiff. Makes enough frosting for 2-layer cake.

PAT'S KARO WHITE CAKE FROSTING

A white, fluffy cake frosting that looks and tastes like White Mountain Frosting and is easy to spread.

1 cup light corn syrup
½ cup granulated sugar
2 egg whites
Dash salt
1 teaspoon vanilla

Combine corn syrup, sugar, egg whites and salt. Beat while cooking in double boiler over simmering water, using electric beater, until stiff peaks form. Remove from heat. Add vanilla and blend. Makes enough frosting for 2-layer 9-inch cake.

ICING

DECORATOR ICING

Try this icing for a durable, whipped cream-like frosting.

1 cup vegetable shortening
1 pound (about 4 cups) powdered sugar, sifted
2 tablespoons whipping cream, about
1 teaspoon vanilla

Cream shortening until light and fluffy. Add powdered sugar, cream and vanilla. Beat at medium speed until all ingredients are well mixed. Blend additional minute or so, until creamy. Do not over-beat.

For icing cake, beat in additional 2 teaspoons cream per cup of stiff icing. For decorating cake, use stiff to medium icing. Add 1 teaspoon cream per cup of stiff icing for medium consistency. Makes 3 cups.

Note: Icing can be stored for week in airtight container in refrigerator. Just before using, whip again until fluffy.

❖

TRICIA'S ROYAL ICING

Royal Icing became popular when it was used on Tricia Nixon's wedding cake back in 1971.

3 egg whites
1 pound powdered sugar, about
½ teaspoon cream of tartar

Beat egg whites with 2 tablespoons powdered sugar in mixing bowl. Add remaining sugar gradually, beating well after each addition. Add cream of tartar alternately with sugar as icing begins to thicken. Beat only until icing is thick enough to spread. Spread thin layer on cake. Continue beating remaining icing until stiff peaks form, then spread on cake. Makes enough icing for 2-layer 10- or 12-inch cake.

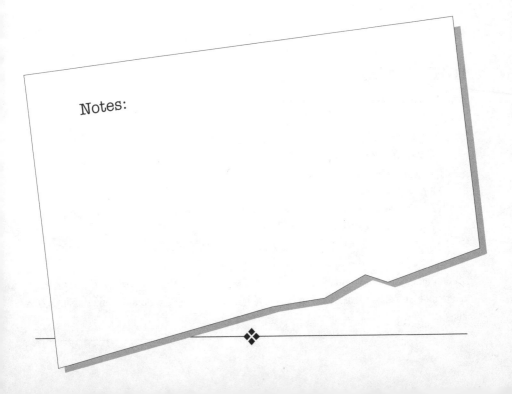

Notes:

SAUCES & TOPPINGS

Clear Orange Sauce

An old-fashioned orange sauce is wonderful on puddings or warm plain cakes.

1 cup sugar
¼ teaspoon salt
2 tablespoons cornstarch
1 cup orange juice
¼ cup lemon juice
¾ cup boiling water
1 tablespoon butter
1 teaspoon grated orange peel
1 teaspoon grated lemon peel

Mix sugar, salt and cornstarch in saucepan. Stir in orange juice, lemon juice and boiling water. Boil 1 minute, stirring constantly. Remove from heat. Stir in butter and orange and lemon peels. Makes 2 cups.

Hot Fudge

Here's a popular hot fudge that remains thick when you heat it.

1 can sweetened condensed milk
½ cup milk
1 (7-ounce) jar marshmallow cream
1 (12-ounce) package semisweet chocolate pieces
1 teaspoon vanilla

Combine milks, marshmallow cream and chocolate in saucepan over low heat, stirring often until chocolate melts. Add vanilla. Serve hot or cold over ice cream. Makes about 3½ cups.

HOMEMADE WHIPPED TOPPING

Here's a topping that's similar to the commercial nondairy whipped topping that has minimal calories.

> *1 cup instant nonfat dry milk*
> *1 cup ice water*
> *¼ cup lemon juice*
> *½ cup sugar*

Chill bowl and beaters. Whip instant nonfat dry milk with water until soft peaks form, about 3 to 4 minutes. Add lemon juice and beat until stiff, about 3 to 4 minutes. Fold in sugar. Use to frost cakes, dollop on desserts or serve over fruit. Makes about 2 cups.

VARIATION:
FRUIT-FLAVORED TOPPING
Use fruit juice instead of ice water.

TRADITIONAL RUM SAUCE

A rum sauce for mincemeat pie, ice cream, pound cake or other fruit desserts.

> *1 ½ cups Sherry, about*
> *1 tablespoon rum extract or rum*
> *1 tablespoon vanilla*
> *1 pound powdered sugar*

Combine Sherry, rum and vanilla extracts. Gradually add mixture to powdered sugar, blending thoroughly. If too thick, add additional Sherry. Refrigerate. Serve over ice cream, pound cake or fruit desserts. Makes 2 ⅔ cups.

NUTS

FRIED WALNUTS HUNAN-STYLE

Hunan walnuts were first requested when the initial wave of Northern Chinese immigrants arrived in Los Angeles.

> *1 pound walnut halves*
> *1 cup water*
> *¾ cup sugar*
> *Oil for deep-frying*

Wash walnuts to remove excess flaky coating. Combine water and sugar in saucepan and cook 5 minutes to make syrup.

Place walnuts in jar with cover. Pour sugar syrup over walnuts. Cool, cover and let stand overnight to marinate in syrup.

Heat oil to 350 degrees. Deep-fry nuts, 1 cup at a time, 2 to 3 minutes. Drain on paper towels and serve at once. Makes 4 cups.

ROASTED NUTS

How about a recipe for Roasted Nuts?

Spread almonds, walnuts, pecans, sunflower seeds or macadamia nuts on baking sheet. Roast at 300 degrees 15 minutes, stirring occasionally. Sprinkle with salt to taste. Cool to room temperature before using. To package, place in clean glass canisters. Store airtight in cool, dry place up to 1 month.

OAXACAN NUTS

Oaxacan Nuts are one of the hottest nuts in our file.

2 tablespoons olive oil
2 teaspoons garlic salt
2 pounds canned mixed nuts
1 package ($\frac{5}{8}$-ounce) chili seasoning mix
2 teaspoons extra-hot chili powder

Heat oil with garlic salt in large skillet. Add nuts. Reduce heat and toss, using 2 spoons, until nuts are well coated. Transfer to large bowl.

Blend chili seasoning mix and chili powder and add to nuts. Toss with spoons until well coated. Store in airtight container and refrigerate at least 2 days to blend flavors. Nuts may be frozen. If frozen, reheat at 350 degrees 5 minutes. Makes 2 pounds.

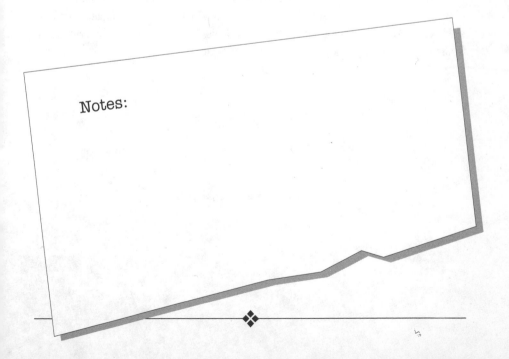

Notes:

PASTRY CRUSTS

OIL PASTRY

Here's an old-fashioned pie crust recipe made with vegetable oil instead of shortening or butter.

2 cups flour
1 teaspoon salt
½ cup oil
3 tablespoons cold water

Sift flour and salt together in bowl. Add oil and mix well with fork. Sprinkle cold water over mixture and combine well.

Press mixture into smooth ball. If too dry, add 1 to 2 more tablespoons oil, little at time. Separate dough into slightly unequal portions if making double-crust pie. Divide into halves for 2 baked pie shells.

Wipe countertop or board with damp cloth so wax paper will not slip. Roll out dough ball to circle between 2 (12-inch) squares of wax paper to edge of paper. Peel off top sheet of paper and gently invert pastry over pie plate. Peel off paper. Fit into pan and crimp for single crust. Repeat if making 2 pies. If making 1 pie, fill and cover with top crust made from remaining dough. Makes enough for 2-crust, 9-inch pie shell.

❖

VINEGAR PIE CRUST

Vinegar and water make up the liquid in this old-time crust.

3 cups flour
1 teaspoon salt
1 ¼ cups vegetable shortening
1 egg
5 tablespoons water
1 teaspoon white vinegar

In medium bowl, combine flour and salt. Work in shortening until mixture is consistency of cornmeal. In small bowl, beat egg slightly. Add water and stir. Add vinegar. Blend into flour mixture to form soft dough.

Gather dough into ball. Cut in half. Flour board well and roll each half into circle 1 inch larger than pie pan. Fit into pan and flute edges. Makes enough pastry for 2 (9-inch) pastry shells.

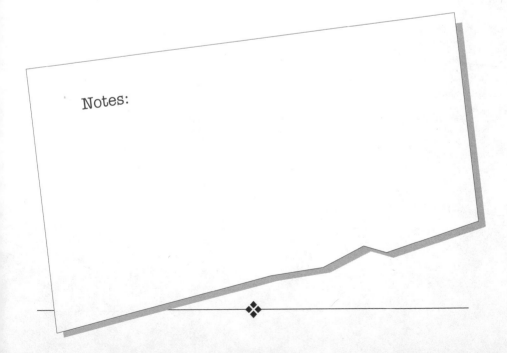

Notes:

OTHER

CANDIED VIOLETS

Readers requested a recipe to make candied violets for holiday gifts or a special cake project.

Sugar
½ cup water
Fresh violet blossoms
Food color, optional

Combine 1 cup sugar and water in saucepan and boil until syrup spins a thread. Cool to room temperature. Using tweezers, dip blossoms into syrup and shake off excess syrup. Dip into granulated sugar. Place on wax paper and dry thoroughly before using. If desired, tint sugar the same color as blossoms by adding 2 or 3 drops of food color to 3 to 4 tablespoons sugar. Thoroughly mix and allow to dry 2 to 3 hours before using, stirring occasionally.

Note: Lemon or orange blossoms or individual rose, gardenia, day-lily petals, or mint leaves may be candied in this manner if blossoms and petals are pesticide-free. Use only blossoms that you are certain are free of pesticides.

CRYSTALLIZED GRAPES

Crystallized grapes are used to decorate cakes.

Grapes
Water
Sugar
Butter

Select firm red grapes. Rinse thoroughly and break into small clusters of 5 to 6 grapes each. Make simple syrup using 4 parts water to 1 part sugar. Cook to rolling boil or 270 degrees on candy thermometer.

Remove from heat. Immediately dip each cluster into syrup and place on buttered tray or platter. Cool 2 hours or more at room temperature.

How To Use Our Recipes

All of the recipes in the book have been prepared in The Times test kitchen, using the quantities and ingredients specified. Recipes serve six unless otherwise specified. Substitutions can be made if the creative urge strikes, but we cannot guarantee success. The following tips should be helpful.

❖ **WARNING:** Although some recipes may call for *uncooked eggs*, the U.S. Department of Agriculture has found them to be a potential carrier of food-borne illness and recommends avoiding eating raw eggs. Commercial egg substitutes may be used in place of raw eggs in certain circumstances. Check egg substitute package for applications.

❖ When you use *eggs*, use large eggs for the recipes. A large egg is equivalent to $\frac{1}{4}$ cup beaten egg. If using jumbo, medium or small eggs, measure the amount.

❖ In baking, unless alternative ingredients are given, do not *substitute ingredients*. One can add dried or fresh herbs, spices, nuts, coconut and other such items, but tampering with dry and liquid ingredients in baked products may destroy the chemical balance and result in failure.

❖ You can substitute one *liquid* for another, such as juice for water or wine for juice, but avoid changing the amount of liquid called for.

❖ When *oil* is given as an ingredient, use vegetable oil unless another is specified.

❖ Use your own judgment and preferred methods for *blending, mixing, cutting or grinding*. You might want to use a food processor for blending or grinding or an electric mixer with a dough hook to avoid kneading by hand.

❖ *Cooked measurements* are different than uncooked. For example, 1 cup of uncooked rice will yield double the amount of cooked rice.

❖ **WARNING:** Be cautious when *igniting alcohol*. Keep hands, face, dish towels and loose clothing away from the flame. Use extra-long matches or lighter extensions when igniting liquids. Never place wine bottles or other alcoholic beverages near flames. Never pour their contents on food when the food is near a flame.

❖ *Baking temperatures* are expressed in Fahrenheit.

❖ Use homogenized, pasteurized whole *milk*, unless otherwise specified. Nonfat milk contains no fat and may be substituted for whole milk in some circumstances. Evaporated milk is used undiluted in recipes unless specified. Do not interchange evaporated milk and sweetened condensed milk.

❖ Use long-grain, regular *rice* unless specified as converted or short-grain, instant or brown. Follow manufacturers' instructions when cooking rice, particularly instant precooked rice or follow recipe instructions exactly.

❖ When *salt* is called for use iodized or fine sea salt. Use kosher salt (coarse, natural sea salt) or rock salt (salt crystals used in freezing ice cream) only when specified.

❖ *Sugar* refers to granulated white sugar unless specified. Brown sugar refers to light brown sugar (dark brown sugar contains more molasses and is specified). When brown sugar is listed it often indicates "packed," meaning to pack it down to measure. Powdered sugar is also known as confectioners' sugar. Measure without sifting, then sift if specified or if too lumpy.

❖ *Baking* refers to foods baked in the oven at a temperature generally ranging from 250 to 400 degrees, unless specified. Keep ovens calibrated for accurate temperature control. The gas company in your area may offer this service to customers.

PREPARATION TECHNIQUES

❖ STIR means to mix ingredients in a circular motion using a wooden or metal spoon or fork.

❖ FOLD (as in whipped cream or beaten eggs), use a rubber spatula or large metal spoon to blend one mixture into another using a rotating or circular up and over motion. Dip the utensil into the mixture, then bring it up and over the surface, repeating until well incorporated.

❖ MIX means to stir combined ingredients until well incorporated.

❖ CHOP means to use quick knife strokes to cut into pea-size, free-form pieces.

❖ CUBE means to cut food into squares of about ½ to 1 inch.

❖ DICE means to cut tiny cubes about ¼-inch square.

❖ MINCE means to chop pieces very finely, about ⅛ inches on all sides.

❖ CUT IN (pastry making) means to use two knives or a pastry blender to incorporate fat into flour mixture until crumbly or mealy.

❖ GREASE means to brush or rub fat (shortening, butter or oil) on surface inside bottom and sides of a pan, baking sheet or mold.

❖ MELT CHOCOLATE, place chocolate piece in a heat-proof or microwave-proof cup and microwave until melted (time depends on size of chocolate). Or place the cup in a pan of hot water to heat until chocolate melts.

❖ CARAMELIZE granulated sugar, place in heavy skillet over low heat and stir occasionally until sugar melts and turns golden brown.

❖ ROLL, shape pliable dough into a circle with a rolling pin or roll by hand to form a thick or thin rope.

❖ PRESS refers to dough pressed through a cookie press; or crumbs or dough pressed onto a pie plate to form a shell.

❖ STORE means to wrap cooled foods tightly in plastic wrap and refrigerate or freeze them. Stored products are brought to room temperature or reheated before serving.

❖ UNMOLD means to remove food from a hot or cold mold by first loosening the edges, then inverting onto a platter. Bottoms of molds filled with cold foods can be dipped briefly in warm water to help loosen from the pan. Shake mold filled with warm food item to loosen it from sides of mold, then invert onto platter. Or place platter over mold opening, then with two hands (use potholders if mold is hot), lift and invert.

❖ STEAM means to cook food on a rack over simmering water in a steamer with a tight-fitting lid.

TABLE OF EQUIVALENTS

The recipes in this book call for standard level measures of cups and spoons. A measuring cup is equivalent to ½ pint (or 1 level cup).

A few grains	Less than ⅛ teaspoon
1 teaspoon	⅓ tablespoon
1 tablespoon	3 teaspoons
4 tablespoons	¼ cup
5⅓ tablespoons	⅓ cup
8 tablespoons	½ cup
16 tablespoons	1 cup
1 cup	½ pint
2 cups	1 pint (1 pound)
2 pints	1 quart (2 pounds)
4 quarts	1 gallon (8 pounds)
16 ounces	1 pound
1 fluid ounce	2 tablespoons
16 fluid ounces	1 pint (2 cups)

AVERAGE CAN SIZES	EQUIVALENT MEASURES	
8 ounce can	8 ounces	1 cup
No. 1	11 ounces	1⅓ cup
No. 1½	16 ounces	2 cups
No. 2	20 ounces	1½ cups
No. 2½	28 ounces	3½ cups
No. 3	33 ounces	4 cups
No. 10	106 ounces	13 cups

Purchasing Guide

BEVERAGES	TYPE	MAKES
Coffee	1 pound	45 cups
Tea	1 pound	60 cups

GRAINS AND CEREALS

All-purpose flour	1 pound	$3\frac{1}{2}$ cups sifted
Arrowroot	1 pound	4 cups
Buckwheat flour	1 pound	2 cups
Cake flour	1 pound	4 cups, about
Cornflakes	1 pound	18 cups
Cornmeal	1 pound	3 cups (about)
Cornstarch	1 pound	3 cups (about)
Cracked wheat	1 pound	$2\frac{1}{4}$ cup (about)
Cream of wheat	1 pound	$2\frac{1}{2}$ cups (about)
Graham flour	1 pound	$3\frac{1}{2}$ cups (about)
Rice flour	1 pound	4 cups (about)
Rice, regular	1 pound	$2\frac{1}{4}$ cups raw; $6\frac{1}{4}$ cups cooked
Rice, converted	14 ounces	2 cups raw; 8 cups cooked
Rolled oats	1 pound	5 cups or 10 cups cooked
Tapioca	1 pound	$2\frac{1}{2}$ cups (about)
Vanilla wafers	19	1 cup crumbs
Soda crackers	28	1 cup crumbs

DAIRY

Cheese, grated	1 pound	4 to 5 cups
Condensed milk	15 ounces	$1\frac{1}{4}$ cups
Cream	1 pint	2 cups
Evaporated milk	$14\frac{1}{2}$ ounces	$1\frac{3}{4}$ cups
Milk	1 pint	2 cups
Powdered milk	1 pound	3 cups

Purchasing Guide

FRUITS AND NUTS

Currants	1 pound	3½ cups
Dates	1 pound	2½ cups pitted, 3 cups chopped
Dried apples	1 pound	10 cups chopped
Dried apricots	1 pound	6 cups chopped
Dried peaches	1 pound	4 cups chopped
Figs	1 pound	3 cups chopped
Raisins (seeded)	1 pound	2½ cups
Raisins (seedless)	1 pound	3 cups
Coconut	1 pound shredded	5½ cups
Nuts	1 pound peanuts	2 cups
	1 pound pecans	2¼ cups
	1 pound walnuts	1¼ cups

MISCELLANEOUS

Chocolate	1 pound grated	3 cups (about)
Chocolate chips	6-ounce package	1 cup
Chocolate	1 ounce	3 tablespoons
Fat	1 pound	2 cups
Sugar, granulated	1 pound	2¼ cups
brown	1 pound	2¼ cups
powdered	1 pound	4½ cups, sifted

GLOSSARY

Almonds – nuts usually purchased with or without skin. To peel, cover almonds with water and bring to boil, then drain. Cool, then press each almond between fingers to remove skin. To grind, place in grinder or food processor and grind to desired texture. To toast, place nuts in a single layer in baking pan and bake at 400 degrees until heated, but not scorched. Or place in heavy skillet and heat, tossing occasionally until toasted.

Arrowroot – a flavorless starch from a tropical tuber used to thicken sauces and gravies.

Baking soda – sometimes referred to as "soda" in recipes. Use strictly as instructed.

Chocolate – there are many types used for cooking and candy-making:

Baker's German's chocolate – bitter chocolate sweetened with sugar.

Sweet cooking chocolate bars – a blend of chocolate, sugar and cocoa butter.

Semisweet – blend of chocolate, sugar and cocoa butter, comes in bars or packages of squares.

White chocolate – milk and sugar blended with cocoa butter.

Milk chocolate – chocolate made with sugar, milk and vanilla, used as an eating chocolate but can be melted.

Unsweetened chocolate – bitter chocolate from roasted cocoa beans.

Carob – an eastern Mediterranean tree whose pods and seeds are ground into a powder that can substitute for chocolate.

Unsweetened cocoa powder – powdered chocolate with cocoa butter removed.

Instant cocoa or instant chocolate drink mix – blend of cocoa, sugar, milk solids, flavoring, used in beverages. Do not use in cooking.

Fine European chocolate – dark, sweet, expensive chocolates, such as Valhrona, often used in gourmet chocolate dessert recipes.

Mexican chocolate – a spiced chocolate that comes in tablets and is used in Mexican beverages and sauces. To substitute, for 1 (3-ounce) Mexican chocolate tablet, use 3 ounces semisweet chocolate, 2 tablespoons sugar, $\frac{1}{4}$ teaspoon vanilla and $\frac{1}{2}$ teaspoon cinnamon.

Coconut, shredded – dry, sweetened, comes in packages.

Coconut cream – cream of coconut milk that rises to the surface. Available in cans.

Coconut, flake – more moisture than shredded coconut. Available in cans or bags.

Coconut milk – fresh milk can be extracted by blending chunks of coconut with 1 cup fresh coconut water from the coconut. Squeeze through damp cheesecloth or strainer. Also available in cans.

Cookie crumbs – usually graham crackers or wafer cookies are used to make crumbs. Place in plastic bag and crush with mallet or rolling pin.

Flour – Several types are available in markets and health food stores:

All-purpose – used for all baking; milled from hard and soft wheat.

Bread flour – a flour high in gluten content or hard wheat. Available in health food stores and some supermarkets.

Cake flour – a very fine-textured flour milled from soft wheat. Use only when specified.

Pastry flour – texture is a cross between cake flour and all-purpose flour, used in pie pastries to make dough flaky and tender.

Potato flour – fine-textured granulated flour made from potatoes and used to thicken sauces.

Self-rising flour – enriched, all-purpose flour to which baking powder and salt are added.

Orgeat – a milky, nonalcoholic syrup made from barley and sweetened almonds. Used mainly to flavor tropical drinks.

Phyllo dough – also spelled "filo" – paper thin sheets of fresh dough used to make pastries in Middle Eastern and Mediterranean cuisines. Also available frozen.

Shortening – hydrogenated solid fat from vegetable oils or a combination of vegetable and animal oils. Do not substitute butter for oil unless specified.

Sterilized egg whites – when raw egg whites are called for in recipes that do not require cooking, we suggest using sterilized egg whites. Available in supermarkets and health-food stores.

Zest – the outer portion of citrus rind, which can be grated or cut into thin strips.

INDEX

ABOUT THE AUTHOR

Rose Dosti has been a Los Angeles Times food writer, restaurant reviewer and editor of the food advice column on which *Dear S.O.S.: Dessert Recipe Requests to The Los Angeles Times* is based. She is the author of *Dear S.O.S.: Thirty Years of Recipe Requests to The Los Angeles Times, Mideast-Mediterranean Cuisines, New California Cuisine,* Tastemaker Award Winner *Middle Eastern Cookery,* and *Light Style: The Low-Fat, Low-Cholesterol, Low-Salt Way to Good Food and Health.*